Land's End

PHOENIX POETS

GAIL MAZUR

Land's End

New and Selected Poems

THE UNIVERSITY OF CHICAGO PRESS

Chicago and London

The University of Chicago Press, Chicago 60637
The University of Chicago Press, Ltd., London
© 2020 by The University of Chicago
All rights reserved. No part of this book may be used or reproduced
in any manner whatsoever without written permission, except
in the case of brief quotations in critical articles and reviews.
For more information, contact the University of Chicago Press,
1427 East 60th Street, Chicago, IL 60637.
Published 2020
Printed in the United States of America

29 28 27 26 25 24 23 22 21 20   1 2 3 4 5

ISBN-13: 978-0-226-72073-9 (cloth)
ISBN-13: 978-0-226-72087-6 (e-book)
DOI: https://doi.org/10.7208/chicago/9780226720876.001.0001

Library of Congress Cataloging-in-Publication Data

Names: Mazur, Gail, author.
Title: Land's end : new and selected poems / Gail Mazur.
Other titles: Phoenix poets.
Description: Chicago : University of Chicago Press, 2020. | Series:
    Phoenix poets
Identifiers: LCCN 2019049811 | ISBN 9780226720739 (cloth) |
    ISBN 9780226720876 (ebook)
Subjects: LCGFT: Poetry.
Classification: LCC PS3563.A987 L36 2020 | DDC 811/.54—dc23
LC record available at https://lccn.loc.gov/2019049811

♾ This paper meets the requirements of ANSI/NISO Z39.48-1992
(Permanence of Paper).

to Elsa Dorfman, from the beginning

CONTENTS

ACKNOWLEDGMENTS

The author gratefully acknowledges the following publications in which these poems, some of them in slightly different versions, first appeared:

Agni: "Josef Albers"
Battery Journal: "My American Poem" and "More, More"
The Common: "Walking Barefoot, August"
Harvard Review: "At 4 A.M." and "That Was Then"
Memorious: "Rest Stop," "The High Line," and "Early Morning Walks"
Ploughshares: "Blue Work Shirt"
Plume: "Eastham Turnips, November"
Poem-a-Day: "Hall Mirror"
Post Road: "End of Summer"
Provincetown Arts: "The Conversation"
Salamander: "At Land's End" and "Snapshots"
Salmagundi: "Nostalgia" and "There Came a Time"

"At Land's End" was also included in *The Best American Poetry 2019*, edited by Major Jackson (New York: Scribner, 2019).

New Poems

HALL MIRROR

Federal style, two small chips
in the gilt frame, found at a flea market
in the Eisenhower '50s.

Nineteenth-century American lovingly refinished,
loving gift of my mother:
It's too good for you, so take care of it!

Some winter mornings here
the taut lit face of Ethel Rosenberg,
or the ecstatic face of Blake,

punim of my six-year-old grandmother,
arriving stunned and mute from Vilna,
her big sister Lena waiting,

who knew what was at stake.

Oh my fierce mother, sanding away
at the kitchen table protected by newspapers,
The Herald, The Forward, The Traveler,

her little brush, her jar of paste
preserving and inventing the past—
for what?

For me.

For today, half-conscious glimpse of myself
on my way out for a walk in February snow,
with a friend, or alone,

my blue woolen hat, my mirror smile . . .

AT 4 A.M.

Some people have an appetite for grief, Emerson wrote,
and years ago, reading that, I thought, *Not me,* though I knew
what he meant—I'd known people to default to it,

people married to woe, dumfounded by any sort of merriment.
Still, I thought our venerable sage judged *some people* harshly
from his Concord manse, where character meant transcending

the insane pull he'd known when, widowed young, he'd nearly died
of grief, of rending rage. Non-negotiable loss, we know *some people*
seem to thrive on it, they can't be coaxed into the light. Lightheartedness

won't touch them, or delight, its hum negligible, an irritant, a cloud of gnats
to brush away. Did lofty Emerson disdain them for frailty of spirit? No,
but he was done with it, that first loss tempering him oddly into calm

for the losses that would come. The calm that said, *Grief can teach me
    nothing. . . .*
Not me, not now. I know day, when it wakes me, can bring back
endless night. Even here, long uncompanioned, or companioned by Grief

and Joy—the *he* in me—I hunger for laughter, for touch, for tears my hand
can brush away. My work now: to continue learning to absorb the loss
and live. Is that work enough? How can I know who or what can help me
    learn?

I'm a peasant, a humbled Mike Tyson said, *At one point I thought life
was about acquiring things—life is totally about losing everything.*
For a fighter, a violent man, that's knowledge hard-earned, whose things

were bulwark against self-loathing and despair. It's clear he knows now things can't be enough. But I don't care what Tyson knows— or don't know why I care—does his abrasive, cleansing knowledge

touch me? Yes. Or is it its devastating articulation? Living on here, I have what I have, an acceptance of loss that disappears in dreams, in excruciating replays of a life draining away—these visitations,

like falling trees unsummoned come, my night a crushing *yesterday* the lit bed-light won't erase or wish away—

THAT WAS THEN

You have a Victorian sensibility,
my teacher said. He said that
as praise, somehow as reassurance

—but I wanted to see myself an artist,
not priggish, not a prude
in love with maybe Matthew Arnold.

It would be years before midwestern boys
would challenge me
to defend Ginsberg, assuming

as an Easterner I'd not only know him,
but be *complicit* with him,
and maybe Kerouac too,

though so far I'd gone nowhere,
just flown to Winnetka
with a lacy bridesmaid's dress

for my pregnant college friend
Susie's wedding. Those boys
had got Sue back

where slipcovered sofas
were covered in plastic
for good measure and everyone

stayed put and for every guy
a compliant dropout girl,
for every girl a sacheted drawer

of cashmere sweater sets.
It's true, I slouched around campus
wearing black turtlenecks

and jeans and carrying my battered
Dylan Thomas therapists would one day
call my transitional object,

or called it last year. But, Ginsberg!
Kerouac! Beatniks!
And *moi*! Which bewildered me—

maybe I'm one too!—
One what? One what? Years before
I'd actually know Allen,

avatar of freedoms I was still
too unworldly to imagine
then, before mind-blowing *Howl*,

before *Kaddish*, before
he was *om*-ing in San Francisco,
before he was being crowned Prague's

Kral Majales. And here Mr. Rinker,
five feet tall, my first "intellectual,"
who loved me,

wrote on my earnest
handwritten Prufrock paper,
Rejoice that you have written this sentence!

What could I know then at seventeen
about Prufrock or his despair? I forget
the sentence I should have rejoiced over,

and didn't, but never forgot
the evening spread out against the sky,
nor *I do not think that they will sing to me.*

Was Mr. R saying I sang to *him*?
Two outliers after class in the amber light
of a high school classroom—

a tall girl towering
over a bespectacled man, thinking
she was the only brooding one,

miserable in her senior year
at a first-class public school—
What was I going to be?

Dim question then, not even
a question, I, still too dim myself
to form the question.

What could I be, just a pretty girl,
ooh, please please not a teacher
like my mother and grandmother,

or like brilliant, misshapen Mr. Rinker,
stuck so unfairly in the wrong place
with his only body—*underemployed*,

I'd say now, glibly but still aching
for his frustration, for his
bewilderment at my misery.

How he did his best to console me,
girl weeping by his blackboard,
poor girl with no useful tools at her disposal.

How he tried: *But what could be so wrong*,
he asked, how could I possibly be unhappy,
he said, *when you're beautiful?*

Not the thing I needed then to hear
from him from whose life I'd soon disappear.

MY AMERICAN POEM

Your uncle was a Trotskyite, mine a Stalinist. We'd idealized them as we grew up, although—or because—they made our parents uneasy, apprehensive.

When we fell in love, only a few years after the McCarthy hearings, we were so ignorant, we thought our uncles would like to meet.

In Washington, where Allan had worked for State, the senator from Wisconsin shattered my uncle's life.

Online recently, I found the photos of him testifying or refusing to, I don't know, the captions didn't say.

Your Harold loathed Stalin (who had Trotsky murdered), lost his faith in Mao, in communism, and gained the world. During the War, he was the *Newsweek* correspondent on the Burma Trail.

Mine, somehow, clung for a long time to his belief in the Red Tsar and did not gain the world. He was a good man, funny, loving, a reader.

During The Hearings, daily newspapers had to be hidden from my grandmother who'd fled the Cossacks. For a time, her fear was the family atmosphere.

Humane, musical, brilliant, having been entrapped—before he died, Allan was gladdened by *Glasnost*.

Both of them must have liked that we idealized them. (Our cousins surely took their parents' heroism for granted.)

Mine loved that I wrote poetry—he read poems. He liked talking with me about poems.

But he didn't really want to hear about Osip Mandelstam, didn't believe *Hope Against Hope*. Or *Hope Abandoned*.

"A single death is a tragedy, a million deaths is a statistic." Josef Stalin.

Yours became a China hand, a professor, and had a swimming pool. During Vietnam, he was disgusted by our anti-war *mishegas*. His first book was called *The Tragedy of the Chinese Revolution*. His second, *No Peace for Asia*.

You were a punner from your first clutch of words—at twelve you presented your parents with the "book" you'd written, *No Peace for Mazur*.

Trotsky wrote an "enthusiastic" preface to *Tragedy*, though in the later, revised edition the preface was cut.

They both loved poetry, yours to write it, mine to read it. He was proud of me, he made that clear.

One Thanksgiving, my brother at the piano and Allan on flute played *Greensleeves*.

What have you learned, what do you know? he'd ask whenever we talked. Usually, I was speechless, sure he'd be disappointed in me.

When King was murdered, we called my uncle to help the black GE workers. Their union had been denied the right to take the day off for the funeral. He won it for them.

It took some years after we married, when I'd grown up and read history, for me to realize if Allan and Harold hadn't managed to not-meet at our wedding, or ever, they'd have been "mortal enemies."

But that's what we'd wanted then, for our heroes to meet, that's how little we knew.

AT LAND'S END

This garden, its descendants of Stanley's anemones,
flowing, pearlescent—like the nacre of shells,

their offspring mine now, in my yard, fragile
beside the orange blare of Dugan's trumpet vine—

my almanac of inheritances swanning
around my own bee balm and butterfly bush,

monarchs and black swallowtails fluttering,
a sunflower bowing its great human head

toward the sun. The garden's heart, the lilies,
its consoling perfumes, the *richesse* of memory. . . .

What would they say today, I wonder, our Old Ones—

Stanley, ancient and clear-eyed, ready to jump into action,
and Dugan, irascible, a furious activism far in his past,

removed, really, past caring about much—
yet somehow bracing, abrasive.

Their—our—century long over, and today's news—
preposterous—still somehow *unthinkable*:

a savage clown "at the helm," breaking
the toys of the circus he never liked anyway—

every treasure, every human pact,
tossed aside as if they were created to be broken.

Playthings of the world, mortal, uprooted.

Oh, Stanley, tending your cultivated dune
under the sun of justice, wiry, undefeated, feeding

your annual seedlings. One late afternoon
long ago, a little too early for martinis,

you lay down your clippers on warm flagstone
by a withering clump of weeds—

Gail, you said, grabbing my wrist, urgent,
what are we going to do about Bosnia?

Where did it come from, where does it go, that sense of agency?

You, so ready to drop your tools, compost the cuttings,
compost your newspapers for the garden's future—

The Times, *The Globe*—

as if here at land's end, here on the coast, urgent,
together we'd have energies to do battle forever.

As if we could rescue the guttering world. . . .

WALKING BAREFOOT, AUGUST

The flats mid-morning.
Fussy, little house-hunting hermit crabs.

Razor clams, skate eggs, black mussels.
Sea glass frosted by the tides.

Far out, schooners, racers, sloops—
Serenity of their white, white sails.

Day moon, round, faint, almost transparent,
Hovering in the pale blue sky,

In its orbit still so near the sun. . . .

An old friend, a neighbor, stumbling,
Has lost her way on the sands.

There's always tomorrow.
There's always something left to lose.

Something here is blowing bubbles.
Something's forever burrowing.

THOREAUVIAN

Another eviscerated wren, its sketchy entrails
staining the straw rug by my chair, and though I try

to scrub the blood away, traces stay. My cat's
grisly presentation, meant to teach me, I've read,

how a mother cat provides for her young.
Pearl's plastic bowl of Friskies by mid-morning empty.

Runt of the litter, born in the parking lot of a Stop & Shop
in Warwick, Rhode Island, she's always hungry but fussy,

eats "like a bird" or a vegetarian, catches these fledglings
and only bats them around, toys with them,

then crunches their delicate bones with her needle-sharp teeth,
her ridiculous growl, and it's over. Except for her howl

for my attention. That tiny life's had its minute—
its rush-and-jumble song, kaput.

I execute my tasks, answering the call of the litter box,
of feathery critters to be buried—but,

but I wield the trowel with a rush of love for Thoreau,
responding to the condescension of an ornithologist

who presumed to instruct him to "*shoot birds*" so he could
better study them, then said: "*If you hold the bird in the palm*

of your hand—" and Thoreau interrupted,
"*I would* rather *hold the bird in my affections!*"

—Little world made cunningly, no longer singing.

THE CONVERSATION

It had come so easily
but then she'd lose

the delicate thread
of her narrative

as if a small wooden dory
had slipped its mooring

floating away from the
warm splintering dock

away from whoever
and whatever knew

how to row across
the deep bewildering

lake   aimless   no
talent or adamant will

to change course
only a light breeze to

propel the craft unwitting
alone into twilight

its frayed rope
dangling   scrawling

along the surface   the long
the abstracted story

NOSTALGIA

translucent golden shells
on the cool wooden sill

bare feet, calloused soles
a small splinter in the heel

of the hand from a rough oar
lake of herring minnows

of snappers, crystalline water
we all took for granted

thorns, sunburns, poison ivy
a station wagon before seat belts

its sandy seat burning our thighs
but forgiving summer

everyone there, grandparents
who could remember the Cossacks

never talked about the Old Country
who was being spared—themselves?

I know a child is shaped by
the unspoken, shaped by what

she'll someday need to study
to begin to imagine

but those summers, darkness
was for easy sleep

cool nights so starry
with fireflies and the vast

dazzling mythos of the
constellations—*summers!*

torn shorts dripping ice cream
cones—the flavors—

cantaloupe, blueberry, cranberry
more tart than sweet

harvested from the bog at the end
of Pimlico Pond Road

where, yes, a hummingbird moth
flutters in the ghost

of the mimosa tree as if
that tree's divine perfume

hovers there now
a half century after its removal

END OF SUMMER

I stood on the flats with the sandpipers and the gulls. The flock of pipers was not afraid of the enormous, fierce-looking gulls, and the gulls were unafraid of me.

The harsh cries of those gulls, the piping syllabics of such tiny running birds, the invisible protein they foraged.

Their meticulous little bills, their genius at finding in the biofilm what they needed.

Soon all but the gulls would leave, their season here over, and I, too, would leave.

When I walked back to the shore over tide-strewn pebbles and the jagged shells of oysters and scallops and crabs, my feet had become a child's feet again, uncomplaining, pliant.

Time had gone by, but in those moments, there was no pain. I recalled nothing of grief or fear or despair.

Grief, fear, despair—as if I were sleepwalking, those were not the elements of that August afternoon.

EASTHAM TURNIPS, NOVEMBER

Honor System, the sign tacked to a scrub oak said,
and on the table a rusty tin box with a slot in the lid

next to a pile of dirty purplish-white turnips beside
a battered trembly scale. Eastham turnips Eastham

was once "famous" for, fall staple from the rocky ground
hapless settlers had no choice but to farm centuries ago,

back when there were forests, before the black walnut
trees were felled to build Cape houses and whaling boats.

The last of the turnip farm stands alongside a highway
that never existed when Eastham was all farms. What

else could grow here in the hardscrabble soil? Today, no
sign or scale, just an empty table, a dead patch of grass.

Trusted by strangers I'd never seen, I liked folding soft
George Washingtons through the slot for history's sake

and bringing root vegetables home and finding recipes
to make the bitter delicious. Gratins. Frittatas. Soups.

REST STOP

Past grassy dunes, past Blackfish Creek, the Donut Shack, the boarded-up basket
and beach-toy shops. Past the nurseries, their young shrubs still wrapped in burlap.

Sunday morning, a crisp spring light and hard-edged shadows, here at this nowhere place
along the route from Provincetown back to Boston where I stop to stretch

my hamstrings: left heel, then right heel propped on the car's humming hood.
Goodwill dumpster, painted barrels, an old semi parked askew, empty,

running its motor, its driver pissing somewhere in the scrub pines. And a battered blue
van like the one my friend pulled into a rest area somewhere in Connecticut

last month, and died. Scarred picnic tables, benches attached. Crows. Birch trees.
Fat, green plastic bags stuffed with trash and tossed. *One foot, then the other....*

He'd been elated, he was newly in love and must have felt suddenly drained
or felt vast unbearable pain. He was a quiet man, would trouble no one—

and who could or would have helped him anyway? Is that what he thought,
Who could help me? when he pulled quickly his green van off the road where

state troopers would have found it filled with his silence? Outside,
the loud whoosh of life, of traffic, the rancorous crows' cries. Did my friend

shudder with the awful knowledge before his too-young heart stopped?
Today, here, I touch my toes, not easily but I do, today I fear what happens

to the body happens to the spirit too. Spirals of piss on dry leaves, on early poison ivy,
then the guy zips, lumbers from the wild margin back to the tarmac,

to his warm truck, and is gone. A gray car, one door a discordant yellow,
careens to the open Goodwill dumpster, its driver heaves her bags

of worn-out clothes at its open maw. The crows caw and rant bitterly,
bitter insistence on life. *Be not thine own worm*, George Herbert says,

and I tell myself, *Summer's coming, with sweet corn and tomatoes,*
with morning swims and evening walks, then fall's brief blaze, then icy storms.

Another year will pass, and then another—Where there are no seasons,
no commotions, how does anyone know to move through grief?

THE BREAKWATER

im Michael Mazur, Bernard Chaet

I know, I know this must be a dream,
but here is Bernie, your teacher,
carrying his old brown shoes in his left hand,
waving his right in adamant, loopy figures.
Whose flower drawings are the two of you
botanizing about—Mondrian's? Van Gogh's?
The immortal cells of your argument—
Bernie his funny, irascible self,
and you, your socks filling with sand,
you, laughing, challenging.
Rockport, how many years ago?
Both of you carrying your French easels,
brushes, and primed Masonite rectangles
on your backs into the near distance.
A luminous July afternoon. As I watch,
the happy tit-tat of conversation
diminishes. The tide's gone far, far out.
No one else on the flats, only you two,
improbably sure-footed, side by side.
Sun, highlighting your blue work shirt,
its ragged sleeves rolled, sun making
the breakwater's jagged granite glow. . . .
—What are you saying now?
Whose line are you praising together?

JOSEF ALBERS

New Haven, 1959

When you steal, kill!
he told you fiercely

one New Haven morning
in your cold shared studio

that was how he taught
brutal his wisdom

becoming an artist
you needed to know

would be a ruthless life
you'd have to take

what your art needs—
even theft and murder—

out of that *he* made
his irreducible art

but how could you
so young know

what that meant?
you'd know when you'd done it—

exhilarated—
struck the lethal blow

THE HIGH LINE

That night I dreamt of the friendship of women,

we were all at an opening in the 20s, near 10th,
the atmosphere aspiring to be electric, the gallery

bristling with women, and men looking past one another
more than at the art. Some of the women I seemed

to have known for many years and others many years ago
but only for a short while. We'd never become *friends*;

somehow something had always held me back—
some atavistic mistrust of anyone resembling myself. . . .

Yet that night, I found myself drawn to them, that night
just when I thought nothing new could become of me,

inklings, stirrings of what might be called longing for
home. *Sisters!* I cried, and only one of them turned away

(I'd so often failed her, my sister, in undutiful affection.
Why? What was duty's relationship to affection?),

but several of them came toward me smiling, apparently
fondly, and together we spoke about what we saw on the walls,

lyrical assemblages of pushpins, delicate threads,
rhapsodic words in many languages, scrawled in viridian

blue, phthalo green, and other painters' colors
I never dreamt existed in nature. And on a table,

tall bottles of sparkling waters, French wines,
crescent slices of sweet tropical fruits,

and through a tall window, amazingly, train tracks,
old abandoned tracks flowering now with native plants,

joe-pye weed, indigo, tree of heaven, squill:
the High Line. Yet that night none of that spoke to me,

only she who'd turned her back, her silence I kept hearing,
unforgiving silence we'd passed back and forth

mindlessly all the years of our lives—

SNAPSHOTS

this one   and this one

on a ferry

a toddler in my lap

whose?

someone headless holding a live lobster

aloft

when?

my daughter laughing

in the parking lot

of Pea Soup Andersen's

on the way to—

ah! San Francisco?

Vancouver?

and this one

this one family

reunion

grandmothers great-aunts

cousins like strangers

wisteria in full

like Giverny

almost

you and I

from the back

holding hands

in the foreground

white gravel

and in the distance

gray rubble

surely we're smiling

leaving

where to?

when?

THERE CAME A TIME

There came a time when fate revealed what was in store for me—
I couldn't cling to you or weep or beg for reassurances,
I'd have to become, from then until the end, transformed,
become fierce, I'd have to be the tigress, not the lamb.
And whatever nurses and residents said to us
would be the text of our narrative of pain, of limits.
And reading that text, understanding its pages,
I couldn't weaken, I'd learn to chase the doctors
escaping me down icy hallways for information,
not to plead for any hint of comfort. I knew insomnia
would be an indulgence I couldn't afford, I knew
I'd need hours of sleep to be what we needed.

Those October hours, I read to you from Rilke's letters
to Clara, his sculptor wife, about Cézanne, about Paris,
about looking at art. Every one of those days, I'd choose a page
from Rilke's October a century before, your eyes on my lips
as my eyes had fixed on your lips from the beginning,
and on your blue eyes, your face turned to mine, to Rilke, to Cézanne.
I'd learn to live in the one day, the one night, days and nights
marked by tests, by terror, but also by music, by poetry.
In the dawns I'd drive home slowly along the river,
thinking of the sweet abundance of our life, loving it,
knowing I was helpless to save it. And I thought of Hikmet,

near the end, the things he hadn't known he'd loved, how
on a Russian train, he wrote with joy and rue of all of it.
I loved the dappled sycamores, the ancient Charles,
loved the old streets I'd walked on and stopped on,
the notebooks I'd filled on dream walks to and from home.
I knew you'd come home with me for a while and, like Cézanne,
you'd be at your easel, painting again, like Cézanne, who said,
I am old and ill, and I have sworn to die painting. Like Rilke,
who said, *Surely all art is the result of one's having been
in danger.* And I knew we might forget for minutes or hours
the way that what we had to *know* was transforming us.
Those October dawns, seeing the sycamores, mottled survivors,
shadowing Memorial Drive, I knew their leaves wouldn't turn
gracefully to crimsons and golds the way our street's maples do—
they do something else, patterning the road and the old river
with their own kind of darkness and light.
Their ancient scarified bodies, their bodies' dazzling grays.

BLUE WORK SHIRT

I go into our bedroom closet
with its one blue work shirt, the cuffs

frayed, the paint stains a loopy non-
narrative of color, of spirit.

Now that you are bodiless
and my body's no longer the body you knew,

it's good to be reminded every morning
of the great mess, the brio of art-making.

—On the floor, the splattered clogs
you called your "Pollock shoes."

EARLY MORNING WALKS

In the middle of Commercial Street R complains
that a wispy horse mane cloud

is *marring* the perfect blue sky.

That's what he's saying, *marring*, when I stop.
This is him, shaking his head,

Marring, marring—he's like an old Chinese poet
mourning the loss of a beloved city.

We look together, we compare the offending cloud
to yesterday's luscious cumulus.

Though R's memory of yesterday
isn't what it used to be

he agrees that was one made you want to reach out
and hug it.

I hug him, he hugs me, yesterday disappearing
easily, its clouds. . . .

*

Mary stops her old bike to tell me
about a new form of breathing
that I hear as *a new form of grieving*—

Why can't I remember what she's lost?
What's happened?
Who does she mourn?

I can't imagine what the new form could be—

Oh, what use is what she knows
that I don't know?
What more am I willing to learn?

*

On the flats two gymnasts
in mirroring postures, sculptural,

invulnerable.

The tide out this little moment.
Old wooden houses inherited for generations,

additions jerry-built over the past century
from spit and salvage.

The old order: how sturdy they look—
yet fragile—

dilapidated homes with names

hand-painted, repainted
above the doors by children, grandchildren

Harmony   Sea Barn   Snug Harbor

*

I sat with you this August morning
on an overturned dory

when the tide was out
I didn't know your name

without language you taught me
how to watch the minnows

and the foraging birds

we were a hundred miles from the city,
its rage and fire—

then I walked alone for a while, alone again
as I've been so long

I felt as if I'd forgotten how to look at anything—

the black head of a gull
the skittery moves of the sanderlings

a brilliant kite stalled in the sky

now looking was like discovering I could sing,
not well, even off-key

but sweetly

and though I never learned your name
today I felt companioned

not so much by you
as by the creatures I was learning to watch. . . .

MORE, MORE

More, more, the bird-me trills
More, more, the surf growls
And more, more, the mud snail thinks
Also the succulent scallop
Unsafe in its corrugated case

No, no, more, goes the blue crab
Swimming in the tidal creek
Too late, too late, more, more,
the god-gull shrieks swooping down
to tear at the tender shell

from Forbidden City (2016)

MOUNT FUJI

Hokusai and Hiroshige, my first presents
to you, two linen-bound books that closed
with looped ribbons and faux-ivory clasps.

Decades later we gaped at Fuji from a window
of Japan Air and gasped together in Narita,
a park so immaculate white rocks gleamed

graphic in a river of gravel. Later still
you'd move between the floating worlds of
ukiyo-e woodcuts and Chinese landscapes,

whose surfaces entered you as if it had been fated.
A draughtsman's draughtsman, Hokusai at 70
thought he'd begun to grasp the structures

of birds and beasts, insects and fish, of the way
plants grow, hoped that by 90 he'd have
penetrated to their essential nature.

And more, by 100, *I will have reached the stage
where every dot, every mark I make will be
alive.* You always loved that resolve, you'd repeat

joyfully—Hokusai's utterance of faith
in work's possibilities, its reward, that,
at 130, he'd perhaps have learned to draw.

In Edo then, his beloved Fuji was
seen as the true source of immortality
(as for him it was to be). *Will you*

always give me such spectacular gifts?
you asked me that day—that day
when we were 20.

FORBIDDEN CITY

Asleep until noon, I'm dreaming
we've been granted another year.

You're here with me, healthy.
Then, half-awake, the half-truth—

this is our last day. Life's leaking
away again, and this time, we know it.

Dear body, I hold you, pleading,
Don't leave! but I understand you

can't say anything. Who are we?
Are we fictional? We don't look

like our pictures, don't look like
anyone I know. Daylight

flickers through a bamboo grove,
we approach the Forbidden City,

looking together for the Hall
of Fulfilling Original Wishes.

Time is the treasure, you tell me,
and the past is its hiding place.

I instruct our fictional children,
The past is the treasure, time

is its hiding place. If we told him
how much we love him, how much

we miss him, he could stay.
But now you've taken me back

to Luoyang, to the Garden of Solitary Joy,
over a thousand years old—

I wake, I hold your hand, you let me go.

MY STUDIO

A garage we called *garaggio*,
ten-by-twenty-two, with a peaked roof.
You painted the plywood floor sky blue
with a long-handled roller from Land's End
True Value. With the ceiling fan, a mild breeze
always blew, though when the tide was in,
the wind would do. My desks—two flush doors
you painted white, on wrought-iron stands,
solid and true. Homasote walls you painted
white, too, and seven small windows all new
that opened and closed. I hung bamboo
shades to block the bay view (distracting
for me as it was for you—its marine clichés,
its colorful hullabaloos). Then I push-
pinned my old poster of Van Gogh's room
at Arles, butter yellow, poppy red, cool
blues, and a photo of Elvis the Jew—
not really a Jew but *a shabbos goy*
who, Saturdays, as a nice Memphis boy,
lit gas pilots for his *frum* neighbors
and opened their flues. (When he died
the rebbitzen broke down and wept—
it's true!) Three flea market lamps;
one bookcase from Staples, brand new,
Assembly Required asked too much first of me,
then of you. When we stood it up, its sides
were firmly askew. Without much to-do
I wrote three books. If we had regrets,
they were very few. Now I know

we were the paper, we were the glue.
I'm still at my desks, it's all I can do
here by our little dream house at dusk
when the bay turns lavender, without you.

BELIEVE THAT EVEN IN MY DELIBERATENESS
I WAS NOT DELIBERATE

We'd be calm, we'd be serene, as long as we could believe
in the blue dragonflies and balletic monarchs that
hovered near us in a kind of peaceable kingdom even
while my love's illness menaced the peace in
the summer yard, in the fragile house, in the air I breathed in my
deliberateness. My only stratagem, deliberateness:
to accept our lot in that pathless time. I
thought I'd know what he'd want; what I'd want was-
n't any different. Wouldn't it be, wouldn't it finally be, not
to consider how finite our August? Not to deliberate?

SHADE

Alan Dugan, 1923–2003

A cold April day, five black ducks huddled,
shivering, on the bay, and coming to life, gardens
on Commercial Street we were all indifferent to.

Eight writers in a sort of circle arguing, ardent—
a committee living on argument, fierce, dismissive—
overeager youthful manuscripts, on fire

with the possibilities for poetry, as if we knew
the stakes, as if we could determine the future
of American literature in that sunny room.

Those meetings gripping, intoxicating, then—heaven—
all of us with passionate positions,
and adamant or uncertain, arguing the world.

And there sat our grumbly Dugan (but was he *ours*,
or anyone's?) in a chair apart, the least voluble among us,
hunkered down, muttering, decades past posturing,

if he'd ever postured, insistent, contrary—yet
the least excitable among us—as we all wrangled
for something we were sure was ours to shape.

Gone for good the Gauloises, gone for good the six-packs.
In his lap, page after page of illegible notations
on the yellow legal pad he'd scribbled on all winter

and kept to himself. Kept to himself, but he was *there*.
He'd told me once he'd always lost those battles—
I never actually saw him fight them, he'd read his notes

and sit, enclosed and silent, except to growl, deadpan,
Everyone's writing poems about Georgia O'Keefe. Or,
They all think they know Coltrane. Or,

Frieda Kahlo. Again. The implication:
no one but Dugan understood those three, and, dead,
they'd become drained, conventions, degraded

by callow enthusiasms. *I don't know if he's a poseur*,
he said of one poem, *or if he just doesn't know what the fuck
he's doing*. No exclamation points in Dugan, only judgments

thudding, resounding in the fierce room from the old poet
who in his distant Brooklyn boyhood was by his parents
nicknamed Spud—*Spud*: that boy impossible now

for us to imagine—"*How—I didn't know any word for it—
how 'unlikely' . . .*"

But today, more than a decade after his death, taking a stab
at sorting my papers, I find in a box some of Dugan's notes,
written on the back of a beat-up manila folder, lines

that stop me—that long-ago ephemeral Provincetown day
brought back tellingly in words I struggle to decipher
and transcribe, his handwriting illegible chicken—or rooster—

ballpoint scratches incongruously similar to Bishop's hand
on early drafts of "One Art":

Only 85—a long way to 100,
he writes, and

The darkness grew closer and darker
and he tried to see thru it to the other side,
fearless and undefeated
he died

On his deathbed—fought his sins to a draw
(I'm sure that's what this says.)
Then, a space, then one more word above a list *I've* written

of sandwiches for the committee's take-out lunch,
Shade
and in my tidy Palmer method, our choices:

2 lobster roll,
1 Greek salad,
4 fried sole sandwich
squid stew
3 lemonades,
coleslaw, fries, coke,
etc. etc.

Thinking of his bitter poems we so relish, I hear the same
unashamed intransigent voice in those oddly triumphant lines,
musical, destined for the wastebasket, scrawled when he was nearly 80,

half-lame, half-blind. . . . What makes me think, copying them here,
There is no music in hell—
Who believes in hell? Who believes in heaven?

AGE

I'd study an old man in a dune garden, his gnarly feet
planted in a swath of blue salvia,
pruning a low-growing red rose he called *Europeana*.

Each summer a new project, dear labor, digging,
replanting, weeding, terracing, taming
the sandy slope—still, always beneath it

the lively indomitable dune. Mornings, afternoons,
dusk, the shrill cries of seagulls.
Moonlight, prehistoric. I watched as if to osmose,

to take in the flame of concentration, as if I'd learn
how it was to be lost myself in a saving task.
But you can't choose who or what claims you.

Though sometimes it seemed he'd live forever—each tier
of seedlings a stanza he'd go on and on
revising—it was only that one century, ten little decades.

Ten decades, ten worlds of change, of fabrication
and horror, ten worlds he never tired of.
The garden's gone now, the lilies, the anemones, the gardener

a tiny body in a cemetery's fidgeting sand by
the white eroded markers of Yankee sea captains
and Azorean fishermen. I'd always thought there was no

weight to him, no guilt or sorrow, he was an ethereal spirit,
that ambition had finally cast him off,
stranded him, as if he lacked the heft of a neutrino

and was moving faster than the speed of light—
all worldliness subsumed—
but that wasn't really him I'd been studying, not him,

just an idea trying to form itself, an idealization of age,
a bearable fiction, a world of tenderness
and nurturing where I'd enjoy my books and papers,

my gardens, where what I'd tend would know to blossom
and each death be followed by renewal.
Those were the days I had almost everything I loved,

until it happened the world shook, and my life
whispered to me, *Come closer, Gail,*
look! I won't hurt you, and I had to look—and it did.

ON JANE COOPER'S "THE GREEN NOTEBOOK"

> *There are 64 panes in each window of the Harrisville church*
> *where we sit listening to a late Haydn quartet. Near the ceiling clouds*
> *build up, slowly brightening, then disperse, till the evening sky*
> *glistens like the pink inside of a shell over uncropped grass,*
> *over a few slant graves. . . .*

Reading Jane's midsummer poem,
I'm in the New England church, listening to late music of Haydn.
Light, pouring through 64-paned windows (was she 64?), suffuses the
   chapel.
The poem at once celebratory (nature, and art) and valedictory
(*late, evening, hollows, scurry of leaves,* etc.).

In here, it is early evening, sunset. Indoors and outdoors
fused by light, ceiling and sky one and the same.
Exterior, interior, painted by the same hand. Jane's eye moves
from acknowledgment of evening, its pearlescent glow,
to the few, askew graves

and the untended grass in the churchyard.
The ceiling, of "brightening" clouds, nature itself as chapel,
chapel as nature,
and late Haydn—probing, inventive, a little dark—
now a kind of hymn to nature.

The mind's eye takes it in, the ear and heart.
Outside, a late July landscape, a pond's arena of density, attrition,
its growth decomposing, its watery depths a deep brown.
Water lilies, early June blossomers,
now at their peak, bronze and muscular. Ethereality

not part of the green notebook's natural world. Jane's point of view shifts,
from the peace of the church interior,
out to the life she can only, in this moment, imagine.
Youthful figures on a float yet also floating, the heat of summer
an atmosphere so natural to them

that it *breathes them*. Sensuality, dense, heated, suspended,
floating toward fate. The midsummer of youth.

Is there wistfulness in her voice?
I don't think so,
although a wise friend says to me it's really about death. I feel, rather,

an appetite for, an awareness, and appreciation of,
bodily and aesthetic pleasures—and for the temporality—
of the season. And more,
a kind of praise song for the world she's taking in,
and being taken in by,

that reminds me of Lorca's "Green, I Love You Green"
and Marvell's *"Annihilating all that's made*
To a green thought in a green shade . . ."

Greenness is all.
But is it all?
No.
Light and darkness. Joy and grief. Life, and attrition.
And unfashionably, beauty—a beauty about to be ravished

I find ravishing.

> *Nameless. Slowly gathering. . . . It seems I am on the edge*
> *of discovering the green notebook containing all the poems of my life,*
> *I mean the ones I never wrote. . . .*

63

Here, the anonymity and therefore, maybe, the universality of the floating
      figures,
what the poets sees and what she imagines. And namelessness moves her
to her work of naming, work she has spent her life shaping,
deepening, perfecting; to the sense of work
yet to be written.

That line break (*my life, / I mean*)
first implying the notebook is the collection of her life's work—
then undoing the achievement: everything
in the green notebook, her life's work,
is unwritten.

So all this time of the poem, has the poet been reading the world,
experiencing the greenness of it *as* the notebook
containing all the poems she never wrote?
Rueful, a melancholy idea.
Annihilating.

The notebook is under my fingers. I read. My companions read.
Has she not captured its greenness?
No—but she's on the verge of it,
of transcribing what her fingers, her senses have discovered.

As if it were braille and she could, suddenly, read braille,
the notebook under her fingers. She reads, companioned and yet solitary.
The life of the artist, the life of making,
surely is ongoing.

Beginnings are a gift!
She's in it now, and in the poem. Time is unhurried, no, urgent,
hurrying, music is in the air: *Now thunder joins in,*
scurry of leaves. . . .

PHILIP GUSTON

Everything, he said,
has a form,
even doubt has a form,

he said, walking away
from class,
the painting students

all puzzlement
at their easels, left there,
with a week

to wonder.
Class over, but he, still
teaching.

On Comm Ave
a blue parked truck
with bright red lettering—

Look at that,
He said, *Look*
at that.

THE 70S

901 Broadway, for Juan Downey

Even the miniature dachshunds were stoned
when they sank their teeth into our ankles,
and we were stoned, too, just from riding
up two floors from our illegal loft

to Juan's, where he was growing corn
and raising bees for his museum show.
His bees flew from Broadway to Gramercy Park
for pollen—or that was the plan. Roaches

loved the rice and beans Juan's table offered,
so he mail-ordered mantis eggs—he'd read
that mantids were formidable predators,
but when their cases opened and the babies

hatched, the immortal roaches ate them
before they'd even had a chance to prey. The bees?
They were delivered in glass vitrines to Buffalo
for Juan's retrospective and installed, the gallery

for the opening gala at the Albright-Knox brightly
lit. Too bright, too *hot*—next morning, the curator
switched the spotlights on, and every bee had fried.
—Oh, and John and Yoko visited one night.

ELEPHANT MEMORY

1994

Pragmatical realists, my friend and I are out
strolling along Mass Ave one reasonable
seasonable November morning, and all of a sudden
a colossal elephant ambles slowly in our direction,
padding north, on its own. Past the modernist
Law School dorms, past the Montrose Spa
and the package store, past the blinking
traffic light and the credit union. Past us.
A peaceable giant a prodigiously long way
from its exotic home trodding our mundane macadam.
Dolorous, like elephants I've read about who
don't forget their dreadful griefs and losses,
the slaughter of their kin. Maybe it's myth they
bury their dead then travel back many miles together
to mourn on anniversaries. Mystics, melancholy mystics.
Tears of the elephants, tears at the gravesites,
trumpeting lamentations, the somber grandeur
of their jungle *yahrzeits*. Foundations of the natural
history museum begin to shake, the ingenious
delicate glass irises tremble, a gorilla's threadbare
stitching splits—kapok's afloat in the airless Hall
of Grand Mammals! A stuffed ibis wakes and grunts
to a dead egret in ancient Greek. What algorithm
leads a descendant of mammoths to journey—where?
unhurriedly through Harvard Square? What on earth
can we make of this sudden elephantine apparition,
this unlikely hallucination Lloyd and I are sharing?
Well, as Saramago said, *it's not every day an elephant
appears in our lives*. Grounded in our concrete terrain,

67

we stand there, humbled, as it sways deliberately,
toward Arlington, leaving the two of us behind.
—(No one with any sense wants to be put in a poem.
But that elephant's been asking for it for twenty years.)

TO THE CHARLES RIVER

Because you flowed through my childhood;
because summers I swam freely in your currents;
because you froze every winter, metamorphosed
to a glazed floor for skating; because I believed
you were the first landing place for Leif Erikson,
although the *World Book* claimed otherwise
(Leif named his new discovery Wood-land,
and Land of Flat Stones); because *you* had trees
and many flat stones, gray skipping stones;
Leif's men found wild grapes and salmon there,
and my father fished from your shore,
catching perch and pickerel and found them
delicious to fry in spite of their little bones.
Because on the Day of Atonement my grandfather
walked from Dorchester to empty his pockets
into you, casting off lint and crumbs for the year's
sins, his good shoes steeped in your waters;
because your dark green trees promised to
protect us, because twice I nearly drowned in you,
and a neighbor child did drown, small body
washed up on your snarled bank. Because
my love and I canoed through your toxic years,
when you'd become reeking and filthy,
only mutant fish and water rats swam in you.
He'd say there's no great city without a river,
and because a Governor determined you
were worth saving, and cleaned you up
and made you swimmable again and lively
with mallards, grackles, American coots—

in our warming world, nearly paradisial;
because an ocean says *Eternity* and a river
says *Home*; because, dear Familiar, I believe
I haven't stepped into the same river
twice, for other waters always flow into you,
and I am always a different person; because
this chilly October I find Devil Pods tangled
among your river grasses, tough grotesque
little seed pods that look like bats or demons
that will always live and thrive in you, and in me.

WE SWAM TO AN ISLAND OF BEES

We swam to an island of bees
and poison ivy, catbrier and low-
hanging blueberry bushes,
of coarse sand we could lie on
to dry ourselves in the July sun.
The only sounds the bees buzzing,
the cacophonous calls of herons.
Inhospitable tangle of an island
we liked, forbidding little island
I'd heard the Wampanoag call *Get Off It*.
There were two others in the lake,
one they'd named *Stay On It*—
it had a battered duck-hunters' shed—
and *Come To It*, a grassy glade hidden
inside a grove of black walnut trees
that had once covered all Cape Cod,
perfect for boat building, perfect
for houses in a deforested Eden.
Some days we'd stay on *Come To It*,
lying peacefully in its soft grasses,
resting for the swim home, telling
ourselves things we wanted to do,
tickling each other's arms and throats
with tender blades of grass, while
across the unblemished lake, a red-
dening cranberry bog I knew honey
bees would soon be working over.
That was before a kind of libertarian
rage fueled the lake's motorized boaters,

before they firebombed the Quietists' floats.
That day, from our island of thorns
and poisonous leaves, the swim back
seemed long, we were drowsy, the dusty
little blueberries delicious, manna.
The bees hummed and investigated
our sun-warmed skin as we lay
not moving, just resting, nothing
to harm us there, nothing in that
first chapter of our life that stung.

INSTANCE OF ME

Hot hot hot, you are hot, Sun,
Glaring all over my east window
Burning, beaming, yellowing

The room. Uninterested in me
Because *I'm* not Mayakovsky
Although I feel you insisting

I wake, that *I* produce right now
Or perish as my uncle used to say.
Brave Mayakovsky, doomed Mayakovsky,

He could sass you, and later O'Hara
(Before they turned forty, both gone)
Sassed you and sassed Mayakovsky, too—

But when I try I know it's just another
Instance of me whistling in the dark,
Me not blazing, me not burning out.

THE SELF IN SEARCH OF THE SUBLIME

I could have just closed the windows when the tidal breeze flapped the shades, I could have gone on working, but those blue shades were so lively, I could have, but I was hoarding up something, my mind a small storage bin of torpor. If I'd even clapped, my keyboard's untapped wordage might have erupted into a thesaural something I could have played at, but my hands weren't ready, they fidgeted by my sides, nervish and ligamenty, their opposable thumbs too twiddly to come to nothing. It's summer, delicious fruition in the air, the screen door open to a seemly ripeness. I could have stretched my spine a little, shimmied some, twirled a hand in a nice flourish Musty Chiffon showed me at Vixen last night, witty Musty trilling, *Honey, why let it hang there doin' nothing when it could be doin' something pretty?*

THINGS

Mementos, knickknacks, treasured junk, set pieces.
Some call them soulless, yet I heard Robert Lowell admonish
his child, a toddler stomping a book, "*Oh no, dear, you mustn't—*
books are immortal souls." Things we might say we "love,"
flea market tables are piled with them—hand-painted trays,
chipped deco pottery; *LIFE* magazines saved in drawers
for their covers—they're little museums themselves:
American photography of our troops at Normandy,
dead soldiers, flotsam, washed ashore; the Dionne Quints,
five little girls in white dresses, caged in Quintland, their Ontario
yard, for tourists and their cameras; *LIFE*, declaring without shame:
THERE IS A CASE FOR INTERPLANETARY SAUCERS
(Marilyn's on that cover). Prowling the daytime drive-in's aisles
at the flea, in the summer sun, I go into a classic hunter's crouch,
walk on the balls of my feet, my arms outstretched,
my fingertips metal detectors for Sunday's hidden coin.
Dusty broken useless. My closets full of things, my shelves
overflow with LPs, snapshots, Bakelite boxes that held
monogrammed playing cards—someone else's monogram—
or unfiltered cigarettes; my grandmother's stereopticons,
scenes of the vast Grand Canyon with tiny human figures
for perspective; my grandfather's tefillin in a blue velvet
drawstring bag. Old piles of books, papers, drafts,
catalogues, magazines—what's a bedside floor for?—
notebooks, science articles torn jagged from the *Times*,
and also book reviews, passionate or sardonic dicta
about what? by whom? Handle bags from long-closed bookstores,
mugs with jokes or slogans holding inkless pens, wood rulers,
random screws and nails. Grandfather's pencil stub marked

Aid to the Jewish Blind, his arthritic hand held it to dial the phone,
its eraser petrified. Mother preached collecting was the only cure
for depression—she couldn't think it was a symptom,
didn't believe anyway in depression. Earmuffs, bell-bottoms,
campaign buttons. Matchbooks from vanished restaurants,
cool restaurants with ashtrays, with smokers. An embossed
plumber's card from Pasadena touts *Miranda the Plumber—*
You Don't Have to Live with a Drip! A small bamboo rat carved
so delicately it's hard to imagine the tool, the carver's hand;
two blackened Senufo masks, displaced, implacable on the wall.
Things, things—Uncle Harold's tragedy of the Chinese revolution,
No Peace for Asia; the last biography of Harry S. Truman,
and Harry Blackmun's; the scathing pleasure of Philip Roth,
of stirring unsentimental Willa Cather's America; a battered
Amphigorey; my childhood copy of *Struwwelpeter*, Johnny
Head-in-Air, who finally walked right off a pier and drowned,
the point being it served him right, translated from the German.
And all this, all this poetry, my friends', the challenging dead,
unalphabetized life's blood, positioned to be rediscovered.
An inventory of them alone would take a thousand pages.
But who on this green earth would type it? And why? And when?
(*So many* things *in your poems*, one friend said to me, disdainfully,
I thought. . . .) Your steel tool-case with molded grooves to fit
each mystifying tool. Drill bits, Phillips heads, brushes, tubes
of color, drying . . . Art—the walls, the closets, the flat files—
humming its demanding song. Or not *just* demanding, generous.
Secretly, in the dark companioning me. Things *aren't* company,
I know that, or ideas, or moral currencies, although they feel like
company when I hold them, I look at them, I know they're here
except in dreams, except in dreams. Loving them, touching them,
keeping them, I'd like to think they love me back. Here are your
shirts, and your hand-sharpened pencils—this blue-gray one
impressed with a haiku by Basho, *With dewdrops dripping /*
I somehow wish I could wash / this perishing world.

FAMILY CRUCIBLE

For seven years, my sister has refused to speak to me.
It's biblical—
but are these the lean years, or the fat?

The one time we had Christmas at her house,
she seated me
in a corner away from the rest of the family,

at a little triangular telephone table.
—Who would I call?
I brought the bagels! I *made* a pie!

So I rebelled and moved my plate and cup near
to my nephew;
we sat by the burning Yule log video—

a mirage of coziness, without warmth.

He wanted to talk with me about Walt Whitman;
I was thinking,
If you want me look for me under your boot soles!

That's when my sister decided to make shunning me official—
she announced it
with magisterial authority to the flummoxed gathering.

One side of the family always had a penchant for hostilities.

But when I think about one of us dying, I'm uneasy
about my sister.
I worry there's a gesture I ought to make,

something that calls for largeness of heart
or, failing that,
something harder, a willingness to "engage"?

Should I rue my puzzling role in this estrangement?
A voice tells me,
Just let it go, the voice of one no longer here,

the one who thought I could do no wrong.

I think she hates me—and longs for me to love her.
Would it be wrong
to rob her the pleasure of shunning me—

me, her *nemesis*—and blaming me for the shun?

GRIEF

Don't speak to me of heartbreak, I have an argument
with habits of metaphor—it's not the heart

In April I brought tulips white
pale green and orange in from the garden

you mean but the ineffable—character soul
locus of feeling—don't tell me that muscle

and with his fine pen he drew page after
page of delicate ravishing tulips

is made whole by breaking—the thready beat
made stronger if ravaged, then repaired

In June plush peonies named for Paean
the physician to ancient gods

Could we salvage joy from each day loosening
Then July I brought the overabundance

of the Asiatic lily's perfume
our ravenous hold on the world—

his hand transfigured the rich ivory paper
Where could it be written

to a garden-room various edenic alive
why would anyone say, why would

a rabbi teach, the heart survives by breaking?
August now and great maples tall oaks darken

and cool the garden so flowers know not to thrive
that in black ink my love may still shine bright

from Figures in a Landscape (2011)

FIGURES IN A LANDSCAPE

March 2009

We were two figures in a landscape,
in the middle distance, in summer.

In the foreground, twisty olive trees,
a mild wind made the little dry leaves tremble.

Then, of course, the horizon,
the radiant blue sky.

(The maker was hungry for light,
light silvered the leaves, a stream.)

I liked to think, for your sake,
the scene was Italian, 17th century. . . .

Viewed from here, we resembled one another
though in truth we were unalike—

and we were tiny, he'd kept us small
so the painting would be landscape, not anecdote.

We were *made* things, deftly assembled
but beginning to show wear—

you, muscular, sculptural,
and I was I, we were different, we had a story.

On good days we found comedy in that,
pratfalls and also great sadness.

Sun moved across the sky and lowered
until you, then I, were in shadow, bereft.

The Renaissance had ended—
we'd long known we were mortal.

In shadow, I held the wild daisies and cosmos
we'd been gathering for the table.

Then the sky behind us pinked and enflamed
the landscape where we were left

to our own reinvention, two silhouettes
who still had places they meant to travel,

who were not abstractions—had you pricked them
they'd have bled, alizarin crimson.

I wanted to walk by myself awhile
but I'd always been afraid to lose you

and the naked olive groves were hovering
as if to surround you.

That was the problem:
I craved loneliness; I needed the warmth of love.

If no one looks at us, do we or don't we disappear?
The landscape would survive without us.

When you're in it, it's not landscape
any more than the horizon's a line you can stand on.

HERMIT

In ancient Greece, a man could withdraw into the desert
to praise his gods in solitude—

he'd live out his days by himself in a cave of sand.
Eremos, Greek for desert—you could look it up.

Hermit crabs live mostly alone
in their self-chosen hermitages, they learn young

to muscle their soft asymmetrical bodies
into abandoned mollusk shells.

Without shells, those inadequate bodies
wouldn't have survived the centuries,

so they tuck their abdomens and weak back legs inside
the burden they'll carry on their backs.

It was Aristotle who first observed
they could move from one shell to another.

But sometimes a hermit crab is social—
sometimes a sandworm, a ragworm,

will live with it inside a snail shell.
And sometimes when the crab outgrows its shell

it will remove its odd companion
and bring it along to a new larger shell.

(The Greeks who taught the Western world
what could be achieved by living together

were also the first in that world to work out
a philosophical justification for living alone.)

If the home it chooses isn't vacant
it will use its large pincer claw to extract

the old inhabitant—usually a dead, or dying,
or less aggressive hermit crab.

Then it drags its spiral shell, its adopted history,
sideways, scrabbling across the wet sand.

That's where you see them,
when the tide is out, on the flats.

At high tide, the weight of the shell
is lessened by the upward pressure of water,

so he can forage for plankton, algae,
sea morsels on the ocean floor.

Actually, he neither "chooses," nor "inherits,"
the mollusk's shell, he has no choice

but to live in it, to lug it with him
everywhere until it's his time to move again.

No shell he inhabits will be his home forever.
Restless, driven, Darwinian,

where he lives today might not please
or fit him tomorrow. I could tell you more,

the flats are seething with unlikely creatures
and remnants of life where life's been unfastened.

According to Tarot, the hermit has internalized
life's lesson to the point where he *is* the lesson.

And you, Gail, though you seem almost frozen,
are you sure you won't abandon

the crowded, calcified armor of your story,
of what was given, what freely chosen—

THE AGE

2008

For what seemed an infinite time there were nights
that were too long. We knew a little science, not enough,

some cosmology. We'd heard of dark matter, we'd been assured
although it's everywhere, it doesn't collide, it will never slam

into our planet, it somehow obeys a gentler law of gravity,
its particles move through each other. We'd begun to understand

it shouldn't frighten us that we were the universe's debris,
or that when we look up at the stars, we're really looking back.

It was hard to like what we knew. We wanted to live
in the present, but it was dark. Ignorance

was one of our consolations. The universe was expanding
at an accelerating rate, we'd been told we were not at its center,

that it had no center. And how look forward with hope,
if not by looking up? I told the others we ought to study

history again, history teaches us more than erasures,
more than diminutions, there'd be something for us there.

I also dared to say we could begin to work at things again,
to make things, that I thought the hours of light would lengthen,

that nature still works that way. We would have a future.
Up to then we'd been observing anniversaries only

of mistakes and catastrophes, the darkness seemed to
blanket, to contain our terrible shame. I don't know

if anyone listened to me, it doesn't matter. Gradually,
afternoons began seeping back. As I'd promised, the children

could walk home from school in the freshening light,
they seemed more playful, singing nonsensical songs

so marvelous catbirds wanted to mimic them. Why say anything,
why tell them the endless nights would return? Listen to them,

the name of a new leader they trust on their lips, *O O O* they chant,
and I hear like one struggling to wake from a mournful dream.

POEM

They said the mind is an ocean,
but sometimes my mind is a pond
circular, shady,

obscure and surrounding the pond,
scrub oak, poison ivy, inedible
low hanging berries,

and twined with the berries, catbrier;
pond where I once swam to a raft
and climbed on, sun drying,

warming my young skin, boys—
that century.
They said the mind or they said something else—

another metaphor: metaphor,
the very liquid glue that helped the worlds—
tangible, solid and, oh, metaphysical—make sense;

and now, fearsome beings in the thick dark water,
but what?—snapping turtles, leeches,
creatures that sting . . .

Who were *they* to say such a thing?
—Or do I have that wrong?
The mind an ocean glorious infinite salty

teeming with syllables,
their tendrils filtered by greeny light?
They don't always get it *right*, do they?

No, it is an unenchanting thing,
the mind: unmusical, small
a dangerous hole, and stagnant,

murk and leaf-muck at the bottom,
mind an idea of idea-making,
idea of place, place to swim home to—

No, to swim away from, to drown, no, to float—

SHIPWRECK

Winter, Wellfleet, 2008

Sweet carcass of an ark, the past's oaken belly—
what the sands had buried a storm uncovered
high on Newcomb Hollow beach; a hull,

round wooden pegs, tool marks that tell
its serious age, ribs like the bony cage
of a Great White whale, washed up

on the shoals a decade after the Civil War, a schooner,
archaeologists say, converted to a barge—
they think she carried coal up the Atlantic coast

from an impoverished post-War South,
coal that washed ashore on the outer Cape
to the hardscrabble townspeople's shivering relief.

In a few weeks, they're sure the tides will resettle her,
she'll be washed back out to sea or she'll merge again,
fill with the coarse sands shifting beneath your feet.

Homely, heavy, sea-scoured, why should she seem
a venerable thing, spiritual, why should you long
to touch her, to stretch out under the March sun

in the long smooth silvery frame of a cradle
or curl like an orphaned animal on the hand-cut planks
and caress the marks, the trunnels, with your mittened paws?

Is it that she hints much yet tells little of the souls lost
with her, the mystery of survival, the depths she's traveled?
Has she heard the music on the ocean floor, instrumentation

of Mantis Shrimp, the *bong bong* of Humming Fish?
Why does the day, all blues and grays, feel transcendental?
She's a remnant, a being almost completely effaced, yet to you

still resonant—can anything this gone be consecrated? Experts
have examined the braille of her hull, weighed the evidence
and they declare, *It's another secret the ocean burped up*,

nothing but a blip, a brief reappearance, once rowdy,
rough with purpose, now not even a container, holding
nothing, revealing nothing. . . . But aren't you also a singular secret

Nature burped up, hurled flailing into the air from the start,
hungry for light, holding onto whatever buoys you,
alive, kicking, even when you know you're going down?

TO THE MAKERS

You were like famous cities with rivers and traffic,
with architecture from ingenious eras,

with protest marches and festivals, museums and pharmacies
and criminal pleasures—

all the essentials needed to endure. Reading you,
I re-visit your structures of grids and avenues, your alleys,

I follow overgrown paths,
I re-visit the terror and joy of being lost,

the ways to court discomfort, to dare chaos,
the knowledge of drowning in a pitch-dark harbor.

Tyranny and wars advanced in your histories,
also infirmities of soul and body

were your portion, yet you were not yearning only,
not heartbreak only,

you were not the loneliest people alive.
There was your work, and then, you had one another,

you spoke with gods and heroes,
you cherished your conversations in many languages.

It is true, you were secretive, observers—spies—
but that was as it has to be,

it was only your work you were given to serve.
You weren't mere investigators of useless things,

the pragmatic seemed no more or less
suggestive to you than articles of turbulence

or rapture—strands of hair in a basin,
light in a dusty stairwell

a pitcher of sangria, woe and laughter,
the feel in the hand of a broken thing.

Day by day, your lives were a tumult of beginnings.
When you began, you couldn't know—

this you keep showing me—
where your constructions would lead,

what you made you made from the inchoate,
muscled and shaped not toward the monumental

but toward a form of truth that would matter,
the inaccessible become necessary.

Though I am speaking to you, I'm not alone

nurtured by your art,
even today you animate the minutiae

of the vast, unsigned cosmos,
and though the twentieth century ended without you,

now, decades after your precipitate departures,
your pages are still touched by many,

still touch many,
and the lit screens you never used sing your lines.

BORGES IN CAMBRIDGE, 1967

Bookish, my bookish friend called you, *bookishness*
the failing grade he gave your genius and his own

after your first Mem Hall lecture on "The Riddle
of Poetry." In that afternoon's amber light,

you spoke without notes, your translucent, blind face
tilted toward the high windows; you seemed to be

gazing heavenward, speaking softly enough to be heard
in Victorian Harvard's memorial to privilege

and its Civil War dead, that first heroic generation
of losses that set Brahmin Boston on its down path.

Outside the old "brick pile," students and bikers
protested the war they hated, war we all hated,

their exhilarating noise filtering, unintelligible
through the indestructible walls, righteous and romantic—

like your romance with Argentina's gauchos,
swashbuckling across the pampas, who'd thrilled your youth;

you'd dreamt of wounding nobly with a sword,
then endured life as a Buenos Aires librarian

in love with books you'd memorized but could no longer
read. How otherworldly, how disarming, you seemed,

telling us Cervantes' La Mancha was meant to be
an ordinary place, not princely—as if he'd written,

you said, "Don Quixote of Kansas City"—Kansas City
and Mass Ave, your two favorite American phrases.

I listened as if the SDS weren't racketing the perimeter
of the Yard, blazing quixotically for a future

like the present with its lovely options but without
the dying, the brutal mutilations. Was I really in the hall

then, or tramping outside—the retrospective Gail
remembers both—I know I marched, my fist raised

defiantly like the other demonstrators, chanting
our chants, month after month—*real* to be mattering,

to spill into the streets, to "be counted," to count for
something: absurdly beautiful, the single-minded ecstasy

of a just cause. Now, memory conflates occasions,
it pauses to hold open my two worlds, offers again

the desperate optimistic din, the quiet lifelike love of art.
The war we thought we'd helped to finish never ends.

TO THE WOMEN OF MY FAMILY

Fierce, frightened, fragmented,
my women,

for the flower of hope for years
I meant

to apologize, that it bloomed in me
without nourishment—

or nourishment was the silvered mirage
in the mirror

greeting me one morning when I was young—
fascinating,

and foreign: hope. Whose sunstruck face
was that

but my own? Why did only the men
make music

in our family? One sang, off-key
but all the time,

the other played piano, the clarinet,
the flute,

then the many beautiful instruments
of consolation—

songs, like optimism, that couldn't really
be shared.

What I wanted, what I wanted to want then,
was for hope

to be divisible, multiplicable,
like the lilies

and the irises, and I'd have divided
the corms,

delivered some to you and then planted
them there

to wave for a week in the breezes
each spring.

The tall blue iris in my Victorian yard—
I'd keep

that plant for myself *and* let it blossom
for you,

its gorgeous unfurled petals, a flower
that exposes

itself, then is rained on, breaks,
dies, and yet

returns, tough and unkillable.
My apology,

my desire for you to have this, too,
somehow

was ungrateful, insulting to you,
my mothers.

I was presumptuous to claim I could
fathom

your wounds born when you were born,
hostages,

as I thought, to your century's contusions.
Of course,

you would interpret powerful injuries
in the blind

careless glances of women and men, strangers
barreling by,

abstracted, benign or malignant but
seigneurial

in their conspicuous indifference.
You knew

the foot was in the aisle to trip us,
not accidental.

Who feared more, you, or I?

We weren't, were we, Darwin's worms,
working and digesting,

useful to the earth and its cultivars,

our own deaths always the only goal?
If I thought

that was the way you lived, pain
always arriving

where you'd prepared the soil, the soul,
for it,

I apologize, I was wrong the way a child
is wrong

for half my life, blind not to see in your
forward moves

courage, the great distances you negotiated,
all of you,

not to see the ground you covered. Wrong
not to know

without hope there would be no courage,
without courage,

no purpose. I was mistaken but lucky,
though it took,

I am sorry, half my life to admit
my excitations,

my wishes, my expectations. Lucky
to feel

my own blessed wanting so much,
even now,

here it is—*so wanton, so extravagant!*—
and here I am

in this minute, almost free to express it.

HISTORY OF MY TIMIDITY

Little sister, little fiddlehead, you unfurled early in me,
your leaflets and blades swirled in my cerebellum,
though I would stand in the yard, muttering

Do not forget the plum blooming in the thicket!

When I'd slouch out on the longest legs in town
I knew it was true
what our Lithuanian grandmother said:

there were no other giantesses here like me,
though she watched for Cossacks
from her jalousied window, afraid for us all.

I wore our brother's shirts, mother's skirts,
outsized shoes, my darling Clementine sandals—
"herring boxes without topses." Dear homuncula,

if I was fated to be large, I wanted not to live
in the shadow of something small,
but to be the flamingo flaring on the lawn, tropical,

not the hermit turtle aestivating in pond mud—

What I wanted: flamingoes, and the world
in my little radio under the pillow,
all the lights out, you asleep, my soft-boned other.

I wanted music, jazz, comedy, Allen's Alley,
Digger O'Dell the fr-r-riendly undertaker!
Intoxicating jokes in the nights!

And blues in the swooning nights, and Frankie Laine
crooning to you and me, *No tears, no sighs,*
we both have a lifetime before us and parting is not good-bye,

we'll be together again. O Timidity,
we *were* together, you, my piddling self,
fermenting resentment, you, pissing on my desires—

like those murderous shy people of the bayous,
crouching with their muskets behind the cypress knees.
—Even now, the memory of you shames me,

drags me back to our twinned days, swamps me
in its black waters. Sister I abandoned, little one,
in the day-world I pretended to be you, flaunting nothing

in the no-privacy of our body—but in my internal exile,
something else, a body steered by the rocky story
of its time, wanting the hula hoop, the hullabaloo,

wanting the flimflam of flirtation, then wanting *more,*
high-stepping through the muck away from you,
night after night, to get *more,* leaving you,

you—square-eyed, despairing, watching me go.

DEAR MIGRAINE,

You're the shadow shadow lurking in me
and the lunatic light waiting in that shadow.

Ghostwriter of my half-life, intention's ambush
I can't prepare for, ruthless whammy

you have me ogling a blinding sun,
my right eye naked even with both lids closed—

glowering sun, unerring navigator
around this darkened room, you're my laser probe,

I'm your unwilling wavelength,
I can never transcend your modus operandi,

I've given up trying to outsmart you,
and the new thinking says I didn't invent you—

whatever you were to me I've outgrown,
I don't need you, but you're tenacity embodied,

tightening my skull, my temple, like plastic wrap.
Many times, I've traveled to a dry climate

that wouldn't pander to you, as if the great map
of America's deserts held the key to a pain-free future,

but you were an encroaching line in the sand,
then you were the sand. We've spent the best years

of my life intertwined: wherever I land
you entrap me in the unraveled faces

of panhandlers, their features my features—
you, little death I won't stop for, little death

luring me across your footbridge to the other side,
oblivion's anodyne. Soon—I can't know where or when—

we'll dance ache to ache again on my life's fragments,
one part abandoned, the other abundance—

ISAAC ROSENBERG

A short man, maybe five-foot-four, born in Maine,
given to depression; a pessimist;
he wanted to be a doctor, I think,
but in the nineteenth century, Jewish,
he applied to dental college instead;
stuck with his name, his height, his discomfort
in his own skin. He had a dead mother;
a stepmother wicked enough to explain
his gloom; two sisters, and two half-brothers
who escaped to New York to become lawyers,
bachelors. You never saw Doc reading
a book—he wasn't the British poet,
shot down at twenty-eight in the Great War
by a German sniper, who wrote the Best Poem
of that war, "Break of Day in the Trenches,"
admired by anti-Semitic Ezra Pound
and T. S. Eliot. Ornery, morose,
but American, so without the specific
tribal dread that news—any article
in the paper—might be bad for the Jews,
fear that tormented his wife and others
plagued by their nightmare memories of flight.
A Republican, only historians know why,
a pinochle playing state-of-Mainer,
crony of firemen and cops, most cheerful
where his wife Jenny never visited:
the back room of a station house, a night
of cards, cigar smoke, good-natured gags
and jabs, and then years later, in Boston,

in Scollay Square, bright cafeterias
where men met for pie and hot coffee
and commiseration. Loveless marriage
to the tall beauty Jenny; two daughters,
in the 'thirties the Gorgeous Rosenberg
Girls of Brookline; a "genius" son at Harvard,
a lifelong Communist Joe McCarthy
caught up with (then even Doc came to dread
the fifteen-minute television news.)
—Not related to the martyred Ethel
and Julius Rosenberg Rosenbergs either
but could have been. Could he have entered
medical school, could he have beaten
the quota? Who told him no?
A little Jewish tough from north of no-
where, would he have wanted to try?
Was that the if-only of his story?
He always wore a Spanish-American War button
he'd found in the Boston Common one autumn.
How could he have written a battle poem?
A bantam cock, once kind of a scrapper,
a bully to Mrs. R, his wife, he loved
his tempestuous daughter, my mother,
and his first grandson, my brother. The year
he died—he'd say "kicked the bucket"—
he taught Jonny some Yiddish I'd never heard
him speak a word of, and that way
helped him pass his graduate German exam.

INWARD CONVERSATION

I'm beginning to understand myself:
I exist in the space my cells leave behind
every seven years when they make room
for a new set of pixels to move in.
Myself: a fleeting entity, made of fugitive parts.
In the first cycles, the transitions refreshed me.
Now, not so much; now,
I make the most of my territory
while those mites rush past me, their time up,
and the next crew of aliens debates moving in.
I'm tough, that's what I know. No matter what
molecular stuff's staggering through the door,
it'll leave me alone soon enough,
so I kick my slippers to the floor,
turn off the light and ignore what's coming.
I relax—I'm introducing my mind
to my mind again. In an incognito world,
it's not myself I won't know.

POST-PASTORAL

Look, I said to myself, go sit in the woods
until something happens. Your childhood forest,
that old Eden, could be a library you've taken

for granted and forsaken. The outdoors, to me,
had always been backcloth, a given, but that day
I determined to be a novice, to read

the remaindered world as if it were the World Book.
Go rusticate, I said, the brown itch of dead
leaves is nothing to sneeze at, nor the ingenious

design of acorn caps, nor the rough bark
of scrub pine at your back. So I walked in
and made my appointment to be a student

of those trees, of the red ant nesting in mulch
and debris, and the pale waxy Indian pipe,
a phantom the Wampanoag call "ghost plant."

My whole life I'd loved one twisted beech tree,
my gray climbing tree, now it was leafless,
dry, and tired, and I came up to its shoulder.

Because I'd viewed nature without curiosity
the Latin names in my new field guide
genus and species, and the common names,

the stems and stones and roots, enhanced for me
the living birds and insects themselves,
the invisible rustlings, the mosses' secrecies,

at home as I'd always been in the lives of pages.
But when I began to look, what could come to me
came to me: I saw toads the size of my thumbnail,

so cute I didn't need to know their names
or name them beyond *toad*; I spotted the dung
of a red fox; a white-tailed deer grazing

on foliage in the cedar swamp. I didn't assume,
as I always had, to be loaded with information
was as good as being loaded with wisdom.

One day, I stood in the dappling greens,
trembling with the emancipated joy
a clever child might take in *spelling*, in getting

every word right, the way the world opens to her,
the world feels possible to master. Could that be
how my grandmother felt a hundred years ago

in Maine, a poor immigrant, at seventeen
only ten years distant from the pogroms
of the Old Country, studying alone

each night the math she'd teach to ruffians
and the nice farm kids the next cold morning
in a one-room schoolhouse in the new land—

each day a triumph for her, *learning* a kind
of moral victory over her own foreignness,
her ignorance. But here I was, an urban woman

in mid-life sitting on the hard ground of the mortal
American landscape, vibrating in the tactile
and the Latin and the grand canopy

of Mashpee trees, telling herself, Look, look, look,
and looking. *The question is not what you look at,
but what you see*, Thoreau said, so I went

barefoot down the warm soft pine needle path
to the lake to swim above herring minnows
and stripey pickerel, I saw mint for my tea

and tiny blueberries with powdery skins.
I stayed until late, fireflies, *Lampyridae*,
lit the black nights, and bats—fluttering,

coasting and diving darkly above the tree line—
my old bugaboos cast malign silhouettes,
sinister cartoons on the waning moon.

Those summers, I lived in the beech forest,
fagus sylvatica, the final forest.
A brief chapter, really, naming the mushrooms

and mayflowers, defying jet trails from the air base,
mourning the ugly dying catfish, uttering
syllables that had been uttered for eons

before me in nature's homely vernaculars,
savoring a truly ancient language, alive
with what had once seemed secret knowledge

and would surely seem so to me again,
and then, only then, when I'd begun to feel
at home, when I knew I would never live

long enough to exhaust it, nor could I
protect it, nor could it protect me,
when I knew I couldn't always return,

couldn't always look and see the thousand
browns, the richness of greens, when I knew grief
was part of me and I would bear it, then I took my leave.

CONCORDANCE TO A LIFE'S WORK

Again, air.
Always another answer: *Away!*

Bed, bedroom, bird—black, blue.
Body, book, brain.

Daughter, day, day, day.
Dead—door, down, dream,

eyes face Father:

final floor, friend.
Girl, give good green grief.

Hard head. Heavy home hour.
Know late (last). Leave.

Let life light—little—look long.

Love matters, & maybe mind.

Morning, mother. Mother movie,
Must muster myself.

Need: new night; night; nothing;
Old own pain.
Pale past poems' purpose:
Questions.

Right room, right room.

Should somehow someone stay?
Still street, students, table.

Take tears, tell terror thing.
Think thought.

Tide, time together.
Toward tree turn voice.
Want—wild with, without words—world.

Years yet. . . .

Again, air.
Always another answer.

Away, away.

from Zeppo's First Wife (2005)

BLUE UMBRELLA

Deer Isle

Kai says, "Here, let me fix that, you don't know
how." This elegant mechanism, a present
from my daughter, topped by its own wind hat,
engineered not to turn inside out in nor'easters
or August hurricanes. Ingenious invention of China
and Egypt, emblem of rank in remote antiquity,
collapsible shade, pampering portable sunscreen
at least a millennium before a damp Brit eureka'd
the thought of keeping dry. Bishop's Crusoe
fashioned one on his desolate island, had "such a time"
remembering the way the ribs would go.
Palpable perfection centuries in the making.
Cobalt canopy I left sprung open to dry outdoors,
away from the library's waxed floors. A courtesy,
I thought, and someone's shoved it into a railing,
so one of the little wooden caps that tip the steel ribs
and hold the water-proofed cloth taut, has split.
Now there's a gap in my assurance of shelter.
Ruined, ruined, I think—my small losses
resound in me today as titanic griefs—but Kai—
who makes his art from what you might call nothing—
toothpicks, mussel shells, buttons, discarded books,
garlic stems—who'll find anywhere, in Toronto
or Kowloon or at this island's dump swap shop,
the raw ingredients of his dreamy constructions,
Kai, who knows I'm not "skillful with my hands"
yet hasn't turned from me, Kai, smiling
in his yellow silk quilted jacket, in his black beret
in the rain, holds out the deft hand of friendship

and takes the ultimate umbrella to his work-
bench, carving for me two perfect maple caps,
one for now, one for the future, when he knows
in his heart I'll need another (don't things
always break?)—And won't we two be far apart?

THE MISSION

Soot everywhere. Trains, as if World War Two were our era,
pulling out of old South Station. At every grimy window,
two or three men—their postures grief-struck, heroic.

The iron terminal all my grandparents had arrived at,
their valises and sacks abulge with whatever mean
possessions they'd thought to lug into their futures.

Now I had their copper pans, their Sabbath candlesticks.
Gloom saturated the enormous room—no light motes,
no cappuccinos, no *New York Times* bestsellers. No matter

what the mission, you'd be too proud to fail to carry through. . . .
The hanging clock's hands could hardly bear the inching weight
of time; I couldn't see the arrows move, but if even one local clock

were taken for repair or replacement, we'd be saved from separation.
Were we—was I—certain you had no rational choice but to report
for duty? You shouldered an Italian leather case I'd never seen,

I, who'd polished and folded all your belongings. I touched your face,
you, already distant, aching to "get on with it," and I—I knew
a great hole was being torn in my life, my life that felt like

the kind of rice paper Japanese printmakers always seemed to use—
such colors, such defined images of comfort and beauty ripped away.
Who'd ordered you to go, to cross three continents

and three oceans, knowing the inescapable dangers? Was it
the Secretary of War, that garrulous fool? What could I have thought
to do or say to keep you from the mysterious assignment you welcomed,

impelled as you seemed to be by your headstrong restlessness,
your admirable infuriating insistence on doing what's too hard?
Was it too late? On Track Ten, obstinate, oblivious of your wife

in the metallic din, were you off to rescue, or murder,
a harmless sinner, were you already doomed to end in a dark alley,
iron and soot, by good angels untenanted? *Don't go don't go don't go*

SEPTEMBER

Let those who stay continue their vigil
over the terns and gulls, let them wait
for black ducks and the great blue heron
who'll come back to settle the wintry waters
of the bay whether we come or go,

I'll go now

while Stanley's Japanese anemone blooms,
so low I kneel to view its mother-of-pearl petals
ornamenting my shade two miles from the mother
plant wavering on the terraced dune,
breezy, near the blue bellflower

and the last daylilies,

my old friend nudging a new stanza,
another late season of color from the sand
he wrote the first draft of his tiered garden on
forty years ago, and revises with obstinate joy
even now,

a car and Sherb, his driver, standing by the gate.

QUEENIE

What was a horse but a colossal
machine that sped away with me, so
finally I hung by one foot from one
stirrup and bounced along the gravel?

I'd thought I knew to make her canter
but I was dragged and scraped over
the country road, not thinking, feeling
This is It, nothing ahead for me but hurt

and blood and ugliness—Who was that
Queenie, graceful chestnut giantess,
retiree from a circus, rescued
from the glue factory or saved from

being horsemeat by the kindly father
of my friend Janet, what deliverer
of knowledge, that she—so soulful when
her huge teeth snarked an apple from my hand—

could, in one instant, catapult me,
a dauntless child of ten, from that morning
to this day I steer our car across a bridge
to your hospital, this brutal day I need

no brilliant doctor to tell me what comes
with the terrain, to say there'll be no one
to lift me from the ground, to carry me
to the stable, to bring me uninjured home.

DANA STREET, DECEMBER

As if I had no language
and would begin again
in the linguistics
of infancy,
but amnesiac
therefore with nothing
to say—

(unlike the woman in rehab
who could walk
and walked the linoleum
at all hours, shouting
to no one, I KNOW
THE WORDS! I KNOW THE WORDS!

—all the words
she knew)

I walked,
past a yard
overgrown, scraggly
after the first frost,
a rose—the bitterest orange—
still blooming, piercing
the morning

(My work had stopped,
I thought
forever)

—perfection
or imperfection
not the issue, a radiance
utterly itself,
pale petals tinged
fiery (provident neighbor,
astute, to nurture
that gift)

(I didn't take it)

Not to be thinking
Is this enough, this
moment, the chilled
unpromising air,
not to be wanting more
than I'd been given,
but remembering

last October when
I carried a glass vase,
its rose
lush, creamy,
across my living room
for your appreciations,

how you rose from
the rush-seated chair
to meet it, saying,
"Oh no, Gail,
the *rose* doesn't come
to you—
you go
to the rose."

ZEPPO'S FIRST WIFE

"One of Doc's cousins married one of those 5 brothers, the funny ones, who were they?"
  "The Marx brothers?"
"Yes, them, the youngest, I don't remember the name—"
  "Zeppo."
"Yes, Zeppo. They got divorced."
                    —A late conversation with my mother

"Why should I care about posterity? What's posterity ever done for me?"
                    —Groucho Marx

He married a cousin, or actually, my grandfather's
half brothers' cousin. No one here remembers
Zeppo's first wife, related to my great half uncles
Phil and Jesse, high-living lawyers in New York,
"bachelor brothers," a little unsavory—

they dated showgirls; when Jesse invested
in a Broadway play, he whispered to me
he owned "a piece of *Fanny!*" Their father,
Simon, my great-grandfather, owned a haberdashery
in Rockland, Maine. *Whose* cousin was it

married Zeppo, the blank, born Herbert, smarmy
amidst his dervish brothers, the baby whose mother
put him in the act when Gummo joined the army?
Bystander at his brothers' rioting subversions—
their chaos in a cauldron—the ingénue,

the "romantic lead," never one of the brilliant
enfants terribles. Straight man, no puns,
no double entendres, more victim than Marxian
tormentor. (People who really knew them
said he was the funniest.) But once, on tour

in Omaha, when Groucho had appendicitis,
Zeppo painted the greasepaint mustache
above his lip, roughed up his slick black hair,
donned black-rimmed glasses, and brought the house
down. The audience never knew—*no one* knew

Zeppo could be as unzipped as his zany
unloved older brother. (Was that his zenith
or his nadir?) He never had that chance again—
"*He was so good,*" Groucho was known
to say, "*it made me get better quicker!*"

—Groucho with his zero-sum philosophy:
a win for anyone could only be a cataclysmic
loss for him. So, in the end, Adolph the angelic
demon harpist, Leonard the gambler,
and T. S. Eliot's pen pal, Julius, Groucho

kept the act alive, leering into unfunny age,
with a callow crooner always filling the fourth
pair of shoes. And Zeppo? He was an inventor,
he created a clamping device our Air Force used
in the atomic raid on Hiroshima, then he teamed

with Gummo, real Americans reinventing
themselves, two also-rans, they partnered up,
began a talent agency and thrived.
And the first wife? my state-of-Maine twice
unremembered distant half cousin nonce removed

whose name I find this morning on the web,
Marion Benda—footnote to a footnote—she's gone,
of course, as the brothers are, through the zodiacal lights
beyond stardom and failure, beyond his family's
history and ours of raves and flops. Replaced,

forgotten. Not missed. *Only the hand that touched
the hand*, my mother would say dismissively,
but surely something more, something happier.
Her life not so unlike yours or mine, or Zeppo's,
then: he never got top billing, no one's idea

of the zeitgeist of the Jazz Age—except that night
his brother's biographer uncovered: he came in
first, he was the rage, he lived in an audience's
delirious laughter, lived, not quite himself,
in the roar of its applause. And then, he left the stage.

SEVEN SONS

You knew the Founding Fathers, all five
Great Lakes, every capitol of every state.
When the teacher asked her questions
you always raised your hand, you thought
her whole momentous enterprise might be
an embarrassed failure without you.

You read a book a day, hard ones:
gold stars gleamed beside your name,
a glittering, prideful dance along
one line of Miss Tate's book-report
chart. Those stars always in mind,
you read in the kitchen, the cloakroom,

even on the tarmac at noon recess.
Breakfast, dinner, tag, kickball—
you'd be reading something. Saturdays,
your father drove from Auburndale
to Brookline, to Temple Israel.
You learned the Hebrew alphabet,

the dietary laws, a lot of psalms
and the begats. Sundays, the other
Burr School kids would walk to church,
to Corpus Christi or the "First Congo";
Wednesdays, to Junior Fellowship.
Some of them, not many, were children

of missionaries. They all lived
in the Missionary Home on the hill—
dilapidated, different but not exactly
foreign. Old people rocked in gliders
on a wraparound front porch.
They'd usually stay a year or two

(you never were invited in),
then back to India or Africa or China.
One of your grandfathers was born
in America, the other was a blacksmith
in the Old Country. No one you knew
had died. You had to know everything:

how a scab forms; the causes
of the Revolution; what *amber waves*
of grain were; what sins Catholics cleansed
when they made Confession; the reason
Hannah let her seven sons be torn
limb from limb then roasted on a rack

rather than partake of "swine's flesh,"
rather than forsake the dietary laws—
why didn't she just tell them *Ess!*
the way your grandmother told you?
Weren't they terrified of pain? How could
they face the dreadful punishment?

Why did Antiochus the Babylonian
king slaughter her boys one by one
for not eating pork? Why not eat a *little?*
Was there a difference between "good" and "evil"?
What made her a heroine for teaching those refusals?
Who could you ask? The rabbi said

someday you'd know. Know *what?*
What change could occur within you
so you'd understand the history of the Jews?
What *were* children to the king? To the mother?
Who could explain the question inside
your question? If Hannah and her sons

were right, weren't they also God-forsaken?
What mattered to them more than *life?*
The dinner table had no place for this discussion.
The questions tossed your bed at night;
you'd only wake with more; they multiplied
like the little boy's hats in your sister's book

that reproduced on his sinless head,
each one more extravagantly lavish,
more intricate and unwanted than the last,
no matter how fast he tried to doff them
to the tyrannical king demanding he bow
bareheaded, subservient, like all the other subjects.

WATERLILIES

They were children at a party. The lights
were out, someone's parents upstairs watching
situation comedies. What was the music playing
on the phonograph? What were the children's
names? Were the girls laughing, and the boys?

—*Dance* music, it was music to dance close
to, the basement door was closed, the 6 boys
and the 6 girls were clumsy, ardent
in the dazzling darkness. It was spring,
early June, I think, yes, the magnolia

was blown, and on the river, the large green
shield-like lily pads curled a little, the showy
fragrant blooms of the waterlilies closed
for the night. The luscious white petals, closed.
Where did they begin, the tangling roots—

in the mud at the bottom? The girl knew which boy
she wanted to dance with. That afternoon,
his hand had brushed hers—on purpose?—
when they'd picked up their spelling tests
at the teacher's desk. 100 percent for her;

for him, as usual, 50. He couldn't spell
"balloon" or "cinnamon," but his body's
genius was sparkling, she'd touched it once
at Miss Boudreau's desk. In the dark,
in her fearless body, she danced something

like a waltz from dance class. Her body,
poor pleasured thing, didn't know
what it meant, coming to life as it did,
so precipitously, all its parts fitting,
forsaking its sappy past. The next day,

she and a boy would take a rowboat
out onto a jungle of waterlilies impossible
to pick, their long rubbery stems invisible,
never-ending. On the bank, weeping willow,
wild garlic. The oars, heavy wooden oars.

A Saturday. That was it: one warm inaugural
night's swaying, then the sun's insinuations,
the carnal tugging at fathomless blossoms.
One day only, one day in the epochal romance
of the Charles River, one day of being with.

His hair was yellow, his face the beautiful
impassive face of a Greek god she'd seen
in the Book of Knowledge, perfect, sightless,
and after that, she wanted only to be alone,
she wanted only not to be alone.

AMERICAN GHAZAL

Sometimes a shift in tone is all you'd need to make you happy.
A shade, a shadow—but then you wonder, is *this* happiness?

Heady scented air of wisteria, lilacs, and viburnum
that could drown you through the seven windows.

When you lived on a peninsula, a disoriented shark stranded
in the shallows; you observed her with terror, pity, and pleasure.

May, so ruthless with your feelings: you're fiercely in love
with your two children a tumultuous continent away.

Still, you could swim naked beneath the Pleiades at high tide
and dance barefoot without music, without a partner.

Altruistic surrender—the merciful self-exoneration
of maternal memory—undone by a child's mythologies . . .

You attached a screen door to the children's room;
a determined cat could climb and cling and never reach their cribs.

Although you have not been granted all you craved, you feel
no grievance, only an abandoned nestling's agitation.

If an era ends, who will interpret the last chimes?
A café closes, currency burns. The present's an archive.

Word arrives of Tokyo's crows pecking at schoolchildren,
the elemental smear and grime in immaculate narrow alleys.

The Gemara tells us *Thou shalt observe* and *Thou shalt remember* came down from heaven together. Remember?

Gail, you can't choose to run away—so, be alive to the work in this room. Whatever else you've been hoping for.

RUDY'S TREE

Rudy Burckhardt, 1914–1999

I admire the way he took
    matter into his own hands,
        (he didn't bring his camera

this summer—and when his son
    brought it from the city,
        never loaded it), carried

his wooden easel in from
    its station in the woods,
        the night before, no film

in his old camera, free
    of desire, the calm I imagine
        he carried with him

into the cool water,
    the early morning resolve,
        his long life behind him,

autonomous, various,
    the pond familiar,
        and dark. And now, I look into

the furrows of his painting
    hanging on my sunlit stair-
        wall in Provincetown,

the ridged bark, the deep
    fissures, gray, brown,
        black: a tree all trunk,

tree I can imagine him
    conversing with, around them
        slender new trees, green

summer ferns, a fallen pine,
    twigs, the tender lyric line
        of one luminous white

birch in the still Maine woods.
    A quiet conversation—
        like ours when we spoke

only days ago. Is it a pine?
    A hemlock? The bark
        is rough, articulate,

dense, a texture craggy
    with age. At the picture's
        heart, an inner layer, glowing.

Did I tell him that day
    how much I love living
        with it?

from They Can't Take That
Away from Me (2001)

FIVE POEMS ENTITLED "QUESTIONS"

QUESTIONS

What is my purpose in life
if not to peer into the glazed bowl
of silence and fill it for myself
with words? How shall I do it?
The way a disobedient child sings
to herself to keep out the punishing
night, not knowing that her brother
and sister, hearing the song,
shift in their cots of demons
and are solaced into sleep?

QUESTIONS

What is my purpose in life
if not to feed myself
with vegetables and herbs
and climb a step machine to nowhere
and breathe deeply to calm myself
and avoid loud noises
and the simmering noon sun?
Isn't there more,
more even than turning to you,
remembering what drew us together,
wondering what will tear us apart?
Does it matter if I tell
my one story again and then again,

changing only a tracing of light,
a bit of fabric, a fragment of
laughter, a closed cafeteria—
if I add a detail almost every day
of my life, what will I have done?
Who will I give my collections to,
who would want to use them?
Don't answer, don't make me
hang my head
in gratitude or shame.

QUESTIONS

What is my purpose in life
if not, when there is nothing to say,
to control myself and say nothing?

What could wisdom be if not
a mastery of waiting and listening?
Is it my purpose to become wise?

What is wisdom? Isn't it a pose,
the will refusing realms of confusion?
How would I approach it, unless

I learned to love the absence of speech,
even the implication of language,
so violently I'd remind myself

of a friend who detests the mimes
who gesticulate on Sundays in the park,
and has begun a postcard campaign

to Silence the Silent. She knows
gestures, too, are a part of speech.
Would it have enough meaning for me,

to watch and listen, to touch
the warm fur of animals and the sandy dunes,
to drop handfuls of fine gravel

into the graves of the newly dead,
to learn grief from the mourner's tears
and courage from their squared shoulders

as they return, each one alone
to the limousines? What gives anyone
the daring to adore paradoxical life?

Won't I always yearn for and fear an answer?
Will I someday have the one thing to say
that contradicts and clarifies itself,

and without falseness or sorrow,
without strutting or stumbling,
will I know to say it?

QUESTIONS

What is my purpose in life
if not to practice goodness
I know isn't graphed in my genes
the way designs are programmed
in the cells of a butterfly's wing?
How can I pretend
that the modest beauty of self-

lessness is not a false glory?
Why hope altruism is part of me,
set into the elegant machinery
by which form and temperament
are generated? The saints are boring
and fictional, their great acts
accidents of a moment, reactions
to cataclysm. What is goodness?
Haven't I tried long enough,
stepped on my own heart, broken
my hands trying to pry it open?
Haven't I lain awake, my head
aching with the chronic dementia
of the would-be virtuous? Haven't I
settled on my right to be harmless,
nothing better? Didn't I fail
at sacrificing, wasn't the last time
it worked when my son and daughter
still slept in their own messy beds?
Who did they think mothered them,
without rage or tears, with no ideas
of escape? Now they are thrilling
voices on the phone, they're at home
in the world, they have discrete selves,
there are layers to them, they are like
poems. What will I do from sunrise
to midnight now they don't use me,
why should I take on anyone's pain?
How will I live if I won't care
for anything in this world again
more than I care for myself?

QUESTIONS

What is my purpose in life
now that it's too late for regret,

now that I've apologized
to the murdered dead and the ones

who went with tubes & needles
on ungiving rubberized beds

and the ones who left glowing,
lovers holding their thin cold hands,

compassionate angels hovering
in the sweetish light of candles,

snow folding itself gently outside
over the dry summer gardens,

soothing the streetlights
and the angular cars, and hydrants?

What can I want now but to be
solitary in a white cell,

with only a mattress and table,
my soul simplifying as Thoreau

advised? I know I'll want one thing
on my wall, a framed poem of Li Bai's,

the Chinese characters say the moon
is making him homesick, drunk and lonely,

I'll want 5 things on my table:
a block of woven paper; a brush;

a stone brushrest in the shape
of the 4 sacred mountains;

I'll want to look at a Chinese rock,
small and violent like my soul,

mountainous as the landscape
of Guilin, vertical *jade hairpins*;

and then, a gold and red pagoda,
a ceramic music box—

when I wind a key, it will play
a folk song I've heard only once

on ancient instruments years ago
as I sat on a carved bench

watching huge golden carp
swimming madly in the miniature lake

of a scholar's garden in Suzhou;
it will play in perfect time

for a while until it winds slowly
down, and then the dying song

will pull me mercifully back
to my calm, impenitent room.

MICHELANGELO: TO GIOVANNI DA PISTOIA WHEN THE AUTHOR WAS PAINTING THE VAULT OF THE SISTINE CHAPEL

1509

I've already grown a goiter from this torture,
hunched up here like a cat in Lombardy
(or anywhere else where the stagnant water's poison).
My stomach's squashed under my chin, my beard's
pointing at heaven, my brain's crushed in a casket,
my breast twists like a harpy's. My brush,
above me all the time, dribbles paint
so my face makes a fine floor for droppings!

My haunches are grinding into my guts,
my poor ass strains to work as a counterweight,
every gesture I make is blind and aimless.
My skin hangs loose below me, my spine's
all knotted from folding over itself.
I'm bent taut as a Syrian bow.

Because I'm stuck like this, my thoughts
are crazy, perfidious tripe:
anyone shoots badly through a crooked blowpipe.

My painting is dead.
Defend it for me, Giovanni, protect my honor.
I am not in the right place—I am not a painter.

POEMS

after Vittorio Sereni

I still write them.
I imagine them lying
to anxious friends wishing me
happiness at the end of my years.
I write in the dark, always
in a state of refusal, as if
I were paying a disagreeable debt,
a debt many years old.
No, there's no more pleasure
in this exercise. People tease me:
You thought you were making Art,
you wrote for Art's sake!
That's not it, I wanted something else.
You tell me if it was something more,
or less: I think one writes
to shake off an unbearable weight,
to pass it on to whoever comes after.
But there was always too much weight;
the poems aren't strong enough
if even I can't remember a line
by the next day.

MAYBE IT'S ONLY THE MONOTONY

after Vittorio Sereni

of these long scorching days
but today my daughter
is truly exasperating—
Stop it! I shout—*or I'll*—
and I twist her little pinked arm
slowly,
calibrating my ferocity—

You can't hurt me you can't hurt me!
She's so defiant, glowering,
glaring at me—
but frightened,
her eyes bright with tears—
See, I'm not even crying!

I see. But it's the angel
of extermination
I see, shining
in his black trappings,
and turning ecstatically
toward him, a little Jewish girl
tempts him
to play his game of massacre.

YOUNG APPLE TREE, DECEMBER

What you want for it what you'd want
for a child: that she take hold;
that her roots find home in stony

winter soil; that she take seasons
in stride, seasons that shape and
reshape her; that like a dancer's,

her limbs grow pliant, graceful
and surprising; that she know,
in her branchings, to seek balance;

that she know when to flower, when
to wait for the returns; that she turn
to a giving sun; that she know to share

fruit as it ripens, that what's lost
to her will be replaced; that early
summer afternoons, a full blossoming

tree, she cast lacy shadows; that change
not frighten her, rather change
meet her embrace; that remembering

her small history, she find her place
in an orchard; that she be her own
orchard; that she outlast you;

that she prepare for the hungry world,
the fallen world, the loony world,
something shapely, useful, new, delicious.

I WISH I WANT I NEED

The black kitten cries at her bowl
meek meek and the gray one glowers
from the windowsill. My hand on the can
to serve them. First day of spring.
Yesterday I drove my little mother for hours
through wet snow. Her eightieth birthday.
What she wanted was that ride with me—
shopping, gossiping, mulling old grievances,
1930, 1958, 1970.
How cruel the world has been to her,
how uncanny she's survived it.
In her bag, a birthday card
from "my Nemesis," signed *Sincerely
with love*—"Why is she doing this to me?"
she demands, "She *hates* me."
                                            "Maybe
she loves you" is and isn't what Mother
wants to hear, maybe after sixty years
the connection might as well be love.
Might well be love, I don't say—
I won't spoil her birthday,
my implacable mother.
                         In Byfield,
in the snowstorm, we bought things
at an antiques mall, she a miniature
Sunbonnet Baby creamer and saucer—
a bargain!—I, a chrome ice bucket
stamped with penguins, with Bakelite handles.

I wanted it, I had one just like it
at home. Sometimes I think the only thing
I'm sure I want is what I have.

"What do you wish for?" I asked
a friend, I was so curious to know
how he'd formulate a wish, to know
if there *is* a formula. His list
was deliciously simple, my friend
the hedonist: a penthouse with a concierge,
"wonderful food," months in Mexico,
good movies. . . .

        Last night, you and I
watched "The Way We Were" and I cried—
I always do—for the wanting in it,
and the losing. "It's a great movie,"
I said, to justify my tears. I wish
you were more like me. Streisand and Redford,
so opposite it's emblematic, almost
a cliché. Each wants or needs the other
to change, so the pushy Jewish lefty,
Barbara, should be quiet, accommodating,
and the accommodating, handsome, laid-back
"nice gentile boy" should agree with her
that people *are* their principles.
He thinks people can relax a little,
be happy. If only
            they could both become
nothing, they can stay together.
All her wishing and wanting and needing
won't make that happen. She marches

against the Nazis, the Blacklist, the bomb,
through the movie decades, and he doesn't
want to be a great unpopular novelist,
so he writes badly for movies,
and later, television.

                 At the end
(it's the early '60s), when they meet again
in front of the Plaza, his look—the blank
Redford quizzicality I've learned
is his whole expressive repertoire—
seems to ask, "Why? Why did I love you?
Why do I still? Why aren't you
like me?"

              And because the director's
a liberal, Streisand's the wiser one,
more human than Redford—she's leafletting,
to ban the bomb, in the '70s she'll be
Another Mother for Peace—the way
she wriggles her sensual mouth
(a mannerism that's become familiar
in the years since this movie was new)
I know she loves him or at least yearns
for him, still wants him, which is more
piercing, more *selfish*.

                 This morning, my throat
is constricted, my head aches, I'm always
like this, this movie reminds me you don't get
what you want, even if you're not weak,
or mean, or criminal. I wish I didn't
believe that message so utterly. Today
I need to believe something more useful,
more positive.

Once, when I was a child,
my mother lied to me. Maybe that day
I was too demanding, more likely I needed
consolation—my schoolmates so lucky,
so confident, so gentile. Either
she meant to reassure me, or—more likely—
to instruct when she said (she couldn't have
believed it, the '40s had happened)
that the meek inherit the earth. That was
lesson one of our course in resignation.
My little mother,
          little kitten,
be patient, I'm trying, it's for you
I'm opening this can of worms,
for you I'm opening this can of food.

THE WESKIT

Thirteen rings,
then her thready voice
apologizing:

I'm sorry I took so long to answer,
I had to drag these two big feet
from the kitchen. Well.

I dreamt about you last night—
Don't worry, nothing bad happened to you—
We were together in a cold room,

I was wearing a little weskit,
a wool vest, and I didn't want you
to be cold, so I told you, Put it on,

but you wouldn't—you said
that would make you just like me.
You said, I don't want to be like you!—

After the call, I went into the kitchen
to complain to him, to remind myself
that I only want to be harmless—

but even in *her* dreams I'm rejecting;
to confess I'm afraid
my yearning to be good is only rage

to think well of myself—
like *her* need to give, my mother
who'll stand for hours

at the shaky stove, stirring the pot:
I know you hate soup, but take this,
it's good for you—

and I accept jars afloat with barley
and shove them into the freezer,
resisting the gift I don't want

as if I won't be mothered,
as if I've always been
inconsolable. . . .

I'd been away,
I *hadn't* phoned until morning.
Now, that small purchase of time

seemed heartless—Now,
I felt I should apologize
for *her* dream . . .

Then, as he half-listened, patient
and bored, re-folding the *Times*,
I suddenly saw her dream differently,

as if it were not about my rejecting her
nor about her manipulating me
in the re-telling:

Mother, I thought, you must not want me
to shiver, as you do in the chill
of widowhood.

You reach to cover me
in your dream, but I shout
NO! I don't want it!

I'm afraid to be like you!
I refuse to live in your loneliness,
your bitter spleen!

I stood in the stunned morning light
at our round oak table,
feeling for a moment the remorse

and satiety of one who *is* loved.
I granted my mother her tenderness . . .
But then I thought,

Who is the *author* of this dream?
Must I enter her and
invent her maternal compassion?

or—as I've always feared,
furious with her determinacy—
is she still *in me,*

omniscient mother, mother
with "eyes in the back of her head,"
mother from whom there are no secrets—

not even my fears, not even in sleep;
mother dreaming my dreams for me,
speaking in the old tone

of accusation, tone of sorrow,
of irreducible pain, speaking
my own private night language. . . .

Whatever the significance of the vest,
I could take it, couldn't I—
scratchy, smelling of mothballs,

brown with suffering, premonitory
offering I might be warmed by
if I let go, if I give in.

Narrow, color of dry oak leaves
in late November, tortoiseshell
buttons I see and feel,

why can't I accept it, slip
my arms through each armhole,
tug it across my broad shoulders?

Who else would use it?
Couldn't I pull it from back to front
even though it's tight for me,

even if the buttonholes
don't reach the round buttons—
couldn't I be grateful? Couldn't I wear it?

EVENING

Sometimes she's Confucian—
resolute in privation. . . .

Each day, more immobile,
hip not mending, legs swollen;

still she carries her grief
with a hard steadiness.

Twelve years uncompanioned,
there's no point longing for

what can't return. This morning,
she tells me, she found a robin

hunched in the damp dirt
by the blossoming white azalea.

Still there at noon—
she went out in the yard

with her 4-pronged metal cane—
it appeared to be dying.

Tonight, when she looked again,
the bird had disappeared and

in its place, under the bush,
was a tiny egg—

"Beautiful robin's-egg blue"—
she carried carefully indoors.

"Are you keeping it warm?"
I ask—what am I thinking?—

And she: "Gail, I don't want
a *bird*, I want a blue egg."

GIRL IN A LIBRARY

"... But my mind, gone out in tenderness,
  Shrinks from its object ..."
          —Randall Jarrell

I want to find my way back to her,
to help her, to grab her hand, pull her
up from the wooden floor of the stacks
where she's reading accounts of the hatchet
murders of Lizzie Borden's harsh parents
as if she could learn something about
life if she knew all the cuts and slashes;

her essay on Wordsworth or Keats
only a knot in her belly, a faint pressure
at her temples. She's pale, it's five years
before the first migraine, but the dreamy
flush has already drained from her face.
I want to lead her out of the library,
to sit with her on a bench under a still

living elm tree, be *one who understands*,
but even today I don't understand,
I want to shake her and want to assure her,
to hold her—but love's not safe for her,
although she craves what she knows
of it, love's a snare, a closed door,
a dank cell. Maybe she should just leave

the campus, take a train to Fall River,
inspect Lizzie's room, the rigid corsets
and buttoned shoes, the horsehair sofas,
the kitchen's rank stew. Hell. Bleak
loyal judgmental journals of a next-door
neighbor—not a friend, Lizzie had no friend.
If only she could follow one trajectory

of thought, a plan, invent a journey
out of this place, a vocation—
but without me to guide her, where
would she go? And what did I ever offer,
what stiffening of spine? What goal?
Rather, stiffening of soul, her soul
cocooned in the library's trivia.

Soul circling its lessons. What can I say
before she walks like a ghost in white lace
carrying her bouquet of stephanotis,
her father beaming innocently at her side,
a boy waiting, trembling, to shape her?
He's innocent, too, we are all innocent,
even Lizzie Borden who surely did take

the axe. It was so hot that summer morning.
The hard-hearted stepmother, heavy hand
of the father. There was another daughter
they favored, and Lizzie, stewing at home,
heavy smell of mutton in the pores
of history. But this girl, her story's
still a mystery—I tell myself she's a quick

study, a survivor. There's still time.
Soon she'll close the bloody book,
slink past the lit carrels, through
the library's heavy door to the world.
Is it too late to try to touch her,
kneel beside her on the dusty floor
where we're avoiding her assignment?

AIR DRAWING

What would be strange
in someone else's bed, familiar
here as the body's jolt
at the edge of sleep—body
persistent, solitary, precarious.

I watch his right hand float
in our bedroom's midnight,
inscribe forms by instinct on the air,
arterial, calligraphic
figures I'm too literal to follow.

I close my book quietly,
leave a woman detective to tough
her own way out of trouble—
local color of Chicago, Sears Tower,
bloodied knuckles, corpses.

I turn to him—
who else would I turn to?—
but I can only watch
for a few minutes at a time
the mysterious art of his sleep.

If I touch his hand, he won't know it,
and it's always comforted me
to feel the vibration,
the singular humming in him,
nocturnal humming...

My mystery falls to the floor,
nothing I'll think about tomorrow—
I'm listening for the breath
after this breath,
for each small exhalation . . .

Is this the way it has to be—
one of us always vigilant,
watching over the unconscious
other, the quick elusory
tracings on the night's space?

That night two years ago
in the hospital, tubes
in his pale right hand,
in his thigh, I asked myself,
Does he love me?

and if he does,
how could he let that steely man
in green scrubs snake his way
nearer to his heart
than I've ever gone?

from The Common (1995)

I'M A STRANGER HERE MYSELF

Sometimes when you stop for directions,
when you ask someone who doesn't look
threatening or threatened the way to a gas
station or restaurant, the person stares at you,
dumbly, or seems apologetic or guilty,
and says these words as if they'd been
scripted: *I'm a stranger here myself—,* shaking
her head, or his head, and you're especially struck
by the bond between you, your strangeness,
and the town, or city, changes to unnumbered
anonymous facades, but generic, unmistakably
New England—white clapboard houses, black shutters;
or Texas storefronts—low porches, two-by-four columns,
longhorn arches; or even Southern California,
the faces its bungalows make, the expressive mouths
of, say, Los Angeles doors—and suddenly you want
to live there, wherever *there* is, to belong
in one place, to read the surviving daily,
you want to get a grip on the local mores,
to pay taxes, to vote, you want to have cronies,
be tired together in the Stormy Harbor
Coffee Shop, to be bored with the daily specials:
you want not to be like *him,* or *her,* not the outsider
who's never sure where things are; so you say,
"Thanks, anyway," and find the worn face of a
native who'll point you to a real estate office,
which hadn't been where you were going—
But then, you stop cold, scared, wanting
only your own room, the books under the bed,

the pencils, the snapshots, what's left
of your family, the dead flies on the windowsills,
the exhausted scorched-coffee smell of your city,
familiar as your own particular dust—and you turn
on a dime, shaking off Church Street and School Street,
the allegorical buildings, the knick-knack bookshelves
in the glowing blue family rooms blind to the moonlit
Main Street night, the lonely, confused, censorious
American-ness of places you drive through, where
you can get ice cream or a flat fixed, places where
strangers get hurt, so you jump back into your car
and head out to the highway, until the town,
that stage-set that almost swallowed you,
disappears at last in the fogged rearview mirror,
and you drive to the next and the next and the next,
fleeing that vicarious life for your life.

IN HOUSTON

I'd dislocated my life, so I went to the zoo.
It was December but it wasn't December. Pansies
just planted were blooming in well-groomed beds.
Lovers embraced under the sky's Sunday blue.
Children rode around and around on pastel trains.
I read the labels stuck on every cage the way
people at museums do, art being less interesting
than information. Each fenced-in plot had a map,
laminated with a stain to tell where in the world
the animals had been taken from. Rhinos waited
for rain in the rhino-colored dirt, too grief-struck
to move their wrinkles, their horns too weak
to ever be hacked off by poachers for aphrodisiacs.
Five white ducks agitated the chalky waters
of a duck pond with invisible orange feet
while a little girl in pink ruffles
tossed pork rinds at their disconsolate backs.

This wasn't my life! I'd meant to look
with the wise tough eye of exile, I wanted
not to anthropomorphize, not to equate, for instance,
the lemur's displacement with my displacement.
The arched aviary flashed with extravagance,
plumage so exuberant, so implausible, it seemed
cartoonish, and the birdsongs unintelligible,
babble, all their various languages unravelling—
no bird can get its song sung right, separated from
models of its own species.

173

For weeks I hadn't written a sentence,
for two days I hadn't spoken to an animate thing.
I couldn't relate to a giraffe—
I couldn't look one in the face.
I'd have said, if anyone had asked,
I'd been mugged by the Gulf climate.
In a great barren space, I watched a pair
of elephants swaying together, a rhythm
too familiar to be mistaken, too exclusive.
My eyes sweated to see the bull, his masterful trunk
swinging, enter their barn of concrete blocks,
to watch his obedient wife follow. I missed
the bitter tinny Boston smell of first snow,
the huddling in a cold bus tunnel.

At the House of Nocturnal Mammals,
I stepped into a furtive world of bats,
averted my eyes at the gloomy dioramas,
passed glassed-in booths of lurking rodents—
had I known I'd find what I came for at last?
How did we get here, dear sloth, my soul, my sister?
Clinging to a tree-limb with your three-toed feet,
your eyes closed tight, you calm my idleness,
my immigrant isolation. But a tiny tamarin monkey
who shares your ersatz rainforest runs at you,
teasing, until you move one slow, dripping,
hairy arm, then the other, the other, the other,
pulling your tear-soaked body, its too-few
vertebrae, its inferior allotment of muscles
along the dead branch, going almost nowhere
slowly as is humanly possible, nudged
by the bright orange primate taunting, nipping,
itching at you all the time, like ambition.

WHATEVER THEY WANT

Tonight, my students can ask me anything.
I'll tell them the story of my life,
whatever they want. Outside, traffic shimmers
in the Gulf haze, mosquitoes incubate
in the bayou. My students laugh softly
at the broad *a* of my accent, evidence—
if they need it—of my vulnerability,
a woman fallible enough to be
their mother. And it's easy, I'm easy
with their drawled interrogations,
their curiosity, the way they listen
without memory or desire every Monday,
while I peel another layer from the onion,
the tearjerker, while the air conditioner
in the classroom stirs the fine hairs
on their arms, and I forget the cool protections
of irony, giving them my suffering family,
my appendectomy, my transcendent first kisses—
What kind of teaching is this?
I transport them with me to Maine,
to the Ukraine, they see my great uncle's
dementia, my cat's diabetes—exotica
of gloom, pratfalls, romantic fantasias,
extravagant sleet, snow, sweet innuendoes. . . .
They ask for it, they want to tell me things, too,
Texas stories, with boots, with dead fathers
and shrimp boats, with malls, with grackles,
with fire ants, with ice houses, with neon,
with rifles, and the Holy Scriptures—

Inexhaustible reality!
When I drive home singing past the palm trees
and the tenebrous live oaks and the taquerias,
I'm in the movies, and later, when I sleep,
I dream of my babies, their insatiable hungers,
I give them permission to say whatever they want,
as long as there's no meanness in it,
as long as words taste bittersweet,
as long as they're true, as long as they move me.

BLUEBONNETS

I lay down by the side of the road
in a meadow of bluebonnets, I broke
the unwritten law of Texas. My brother

was visiting, he'd been tired, afraid of
his tiredness as we'd driven toward Bremen,
so we stopped for the blue relatives

of lupine, we left the car on huge feet
we'd inherited from our lost father,
our Polish grandfather. Those flowers

were too beautiful to only look at;
we walked on them, stood in the middle
of them, threw ourselves down,

crushing them in their one opportunity
to thrive and bloom. We lay like angels
forgiven our misdeeds, transported

to azure fields, the only word for
the color eluded me—delft, indigo,
sapphire, some heavenly word you might

speak to a sky. I led my terrestrial brother
there to make him smile and this
is my only record of the event.

We took no pictures, we knew no camera
could fathom that blue. I brushed
the soft spikes, I fingered lightly

the delicate earthly petals, I thought,
This is what my hands do well
isn't it, touch things about to vanish.

POEM FOR CHRISTIAN, MY STUDENT

He reminds me of someone I used to know,
but who? Before class,
he comes to my office to shmooze,
a thousand thousand pointless interesting
speculations. Irrepressible boy,
his assignments are rarely completed,
or actually started. This week, instead
of research in the stacks, he's performing
with a reggae band that didn't exist last week.
Kids danced to his music
and stripped, he tells me gleefully,
high spirit of the street festival.
He's the singer, of course—
why ask if he studied an instrument?
On the brink of graduating with
an engineering degree (not, it turned out,
his forte), he switched to English,
his second language. It's hard to swallow
the bravura of his academic escapes
or tell if the dark eyes laugh with his face.
Once, he brought me a tiny persimmon
he'd picked on campus; once, a poem
about an elderly friend in New Delhi
who left him volumes of Tagore
and memories of avuncular conversation.
My encouragement makes him skittish—
it doesn't suit his jubilant histrionics
of despair. And I remember myself
shrinking from enthusiasm or praise,

the prospect of effort—drudgery.
Success—a threat. A future, we figure,
of revision—yet what can the future be
but revision and repair? Now, on the brink
again, graduation's postponed, the brilliant
thesis on Walker Percy unwritten.
"I'll drive to New Orleans and soak
it up and write my paper in a weekend,"
he announces in the Honors office.
And, "I want to be a bum in daytime
and a reggae star at night!"
What could I give him from my life
or art that matters, how share
the desperate slumber of my early years,
the flashes of inspiration and passion
in a life on hold? If I didn't fool
myself or anyone, no one could touch
me, or tell me much . . . This gloomy
Houston Monday, he appears at my door,
so sunny I wouldn't dare to wake him
now, or say it matters if he wakes at all.
"Write a poem about me!" he commands,
and so I do.

FOLIAGE

Even the man who dozes on cardboard
in the Common, wearing a bright knit cap,
has picked Clover and Ladies' Thumb to stick
in the cosmos of his shopping cart.
These last warm days, wanting to deny
what's frozen and gray ahead, I admire
the star turns of my town's great trees.
Sunbursts, and the alizarin crimson

of our maples' explosions, a kind of payoff
(I want to think) for all the dying,
yet something I'm part of—part of me—
like my feet, planted deferentially
in this old park, my hands red at my sides,
my head nodding and shaking in the leafy air.

ICE

In the warming house, children lace their skates,
bending, choked, over their thick jackets.

A Franklin stove keeps the place so cozy
it's hard to imagine why anyone would leave,

clumping across the frozen beach to the river.
December's always the same at Ware's Cove,

the first sheer ice, black, then white
and deep until the city sends trucks of men

with wooden barriers to put up the boys'
hockey rink. An hour of skating after school,

of trying wobbly figure-8's, an hour
of distances moved backwards without falling,

then—twilight, the warming house steamy
with girls pulling on boots, their chafed legs

aching. Outside, the hockey players keep
playing, slamming the round black puck

until it's dark, until supper. At night,
a shy girl comes to the cove with her father.

Although there isn't music, they glide
arm in arm onto the blurred surface together,

braced like dancers. She thinks she'll never
be so happy, for who else will find her graceful,

find her perfect, skate with her
in circles outside the emptied rink forever?

POEM ENDING WITH THREE LINES OF WORDSWORTH'S

The organ donor who smiles
in the leathery dark of my wallet
from a driver's license

has already struck one woman—
elderly, confused—
who stumbled off a Somerville curb

one January dusk
and became a sickening thump,
then a bleeding body

cradled in the driver's arms
until police and ambulance came.
That old woman lived

to sue the driver who now
takes a different route each week
to the supermarket,

and on her birthday,
in line at the Registry, decides
she's old enough, if not

for a Living Will, then to leave
her kidneys or heart or liver;
the little silver label below her

Polaroid portrait is the Registry's
donor code. She envisions herself
extricated one night

from crushed burning metal
by the jaws of life
less lucky, finally, than her victim

whose two pocketbooks (maybe
she was a pursesnatcher?) flew
in opposite directions

and landed awfully far
from the eyeglasses and left shoe.
All the eyewitnesses

exonerated the driver.
They swore to what she won't remember:
the old woman fell,

or fainted to the fender;
the car was going five miles an hour.
Still, that impact was what she'd dreaded

all her tremulous years at the wheel
which she grips for dear guilty life,
concocting terms of a bargain—

she'll bequeath what she's got in her body
so whatever virtues she lacks,
she won't just be someone dead

unprofitably traveling toward the grave
like a false steward who has much received
and renders nothing back.

BEDROOM AT ARLES

A painting he thought would rest the brain,
or rather, the imagination—

sloped room, chrome-yellow bed,
poppy-red coverlet, his own pictures

hung askew, or painted as if they were.
He'd splash cold water from the blue basin,

then take his blue smock from the peg.
Whole days outdoors he spoke to no one,

straining, as he had to, alone,
for *the high yellow note*. . . .

Decades ago, I longed to be like him—
an isolate, a genius; beneath a poster

of his raw crooked room, I planned
a life, a monk's life, a vocation.

I was sure craziness was a side issue,
like the mistral's dust that whitened trees,

that drove him indoors to paint—
an obstacle yet, oddly, fine.

Now it seems a century's gone by
since I read his daily diary

of pictures,
that fevered year at Arles—

blue cypresses, apricot orchards,
Arlesienne faces. This bedroom.

A century, at least,
since I underestimated danger

and quarantined myself in the one room,
trying on a little madness, a little despair,

waking in the fictive mornings,
not awake yet to light like his—yellows

like sulphur, like lemons, like fresh butter,
not golden, or blazing, but homely—

from The Pose of Happiness (1986)

THE HORIZONTAL MAN

Surely it was too awful to be real. The
darkened library, the buildings full of
empty classrooms, the threatening olive-
green shape of the mailbox under the lamp
at the centre of the campus . . .
    —Helen Eustis, *The Horizontal Man* (1946)

On the second page,
my old professor's murdered with a poker.
His black curls, matting with blood
on the shabby rug,
      were wild and gray
when he lectured to the Shakespeare class
on Sputnik and Ophelia. We'd all heard
of his affairs, and of this novel,
already out-of-print, written by a former wife

who killed him with a pen—revenge
more cruel than alimony
to young things on allowances . . .

When he recited "O, what a rogue
and peasant slave am I," we thrilled
to the alcoholic timbre of his brogue . . .

This reissued mystery
brings the whole semester back.
Fat, and pining for a boy,
I ate and smoked and slept most days away,
convinced I'd end up lonely, and alone.

For Professor F, I studied
"O that this too too solid flesh would melt,"
and earned the isolated A that failed
to keep my parents' hopes for me alive.

I recognize the Infirmary—
it's at the end of Paradise Road.
The demented freshman's dragged there
in the second chapter, babbling about love;
the nurse thinks she's the "perpetrator."

I remember the unwomanly physician
stricken by the vagaries of menstruation—
Is the psychiatrist from Springfield
the one they called the night my mind
was slipping, and the dean suspected
that wasn't all I'd lost that term?

In the spring nocturnes of my sophomore year,
I lay on my restricted cot,
confined to campus for my indiscretion—
my confession. I memorized soliloquies
for Doctor F—"To be or not"—
as if my life depended on my memory.
There was nothing I was going to *be* . . .

My teacher died, exhausted,
in a rest home late last year.

I've read all night again.
This *roman à clef*, with its bloody weapon
on the cover, is like the dream I stay up
to avoid, the classic college nightmare:
a gothic building, and months
of literature unread, the unversed girl

I never stop becoming, dragging
her cold feet through the scrollery
iron gate, past Paradise Pond
to the examination hall silently
filling with victims and perpetrators.

JEWELWEED

We were talking about sex, taking
the dirt road to town, walking
slowly in the hot afternoon.

I hardly saw the fields
shimmering in the heat, the goldenrod's
itchy impressionist glow,

the pale touch-me-not,
or jewelweed, blooming in shade,
so skewed was my vision,

so interior. That day we agreed
never to touch each other,
passing the warm brown beds of pine

needles, the tiny graveyard. My face,
your face, reddened in August's ardent
flush; our hands clung to their pockets.

That conversation seemed harmless—
strange, that I still need
to put it this way—

Anyway, it must have been too far
to town. We turned back at a stone
marker to join our friends swimming

in a black pond deep in our past.
Now I am in the future where nothing
has happened, nothing happens.

What were we walking toward
that prickly summer day,
both of us suddenly guarded,

uneasy strangers, or greenhorns,
or children transported unprepared
to a heartless institution?

READING AKHMATOVA

This morning I went into the woods
to find a beech tree of my childhood.
Gray-limbed, motherly and capacious,
it once seemed to me the only place
to brood over my mournful lucky life.
It was still there, but leafless,
not much taller than myself. I leaned
my cheek on a cool dead branch
and stood that way a while until
my own mawkishness embarrassed me—
the way I always lament these small
inexorable shifts in the ecology.
So I walked down the hill, my feet
crunching in the dry beech leaves,
and swam in the old lake, holy
as the world's past. Only a family
of mallards was swimming there, moving
toward shore until they sensed me
and turned and glided away,
their feet making a frantic stir
under the water's surface.

I've lost no one.
Not my mother, alone today
under anaesthesia, my frail father
waiting here by the phone, my son
and daughter thousands of miles apart,

thousands from me. Last night I woke
again and again, heard my gray cat
scratching to get out, and kept him in.
I'm ordinary—my fears are ordinary.

HURRICANE WATCH

The power was off.
We cleared dishes from the table.
Shutters crashed against the windows.
Below us, in the lake, the minnows
were in a frenzy. Limbs cracked—
one great tree smashed to the ground.
Leaves flew past, pasted themselves
to the panes. Somewhere,
my father was on a train.

The blue walls quaked,
too weak to hold the roof up.
Telephone lines were dead.
We had no batteries for the radio.
Our neighbors weren't our friends—
we couldn't ask them for news.
We lit the charred wicks of the lamps
and watched the wind, and listened:
anything could crash and slide away.
Night passed crookedly like nightmare.

Wind blew in my chest.
We'd waited hours for father,
due home on the Beeliner.
Whatever mother feared, I feared.
Maybe the bridge was down.
I thought of the train twisted
off the rails; I couldn't think.

Kerosene glow from the neighbor's window
might have been stars glistening.
They didn't know we were in a frenzy.

I huddled tight in my bones
counting a million by twenties
to bring him home. In my mind,
the train was a Lionel toy,
anyone could smash it.
1000 . . . 1020 . . . 1040 . . .
At midnight the door flew open.
My dazzling father was home, with favors,
red swizzle sticks from the bar car.
I watched him hugging mother,
and heard the wind,
and kept counting.

FALLEN ANGELS

I almost died last night eating shrimp.
That's how they diagnosed it
at Mount Auburn Emergency after
they'd shot me full of adrenalin.
My heart fluttered, I couldn't keep
my hands still, and I laughed and cried
like a crazy person, my face swollen
with hives, my throat closing.

"I don't look like this,"
I insisted to an intern who
wasn't interested in my looks,
just whether I kept breathing.

Now everyone in the family's impaired.
Even my brother hears whistling
when he walks down his own hallway—
nowhere else. There aren't any windows,
so it's not the wind, and not tinnitus—
his ears only whistle in the one hallway.

We're used to his peculiar ailments;
he's our genius. Last year,
he was sure his face was falling.
And before that, for months he couldn't
read, or see in his microscope.

He thought his nose was beginning
to block his vision. An ophthalmologist
at the Health Plan said his eyes were
"normal."

We're what I used to call
"discombombulated."

To forget our troubles,
I go every night to a different *film noir*.
Sometimes my brother comes along.
We want to see a hapless loser
we can't identify with,
and some stylized violence—
Dana Andrews, grabbing women
too hard, and talking without moving
his thin, cruel lips; John Garfield
(before the blacklist), corrupted
because he grows up on the Lower East Side
and becomes a boxer and loves money.

We laugh dispassionately at Linda Darnell,
plump, coarse, contemptuous of men
as she pours coffee in a crummy diner—
Pop's Diner—every unattractive man
in town (population 4,000), including
Pop, slavering over the counter at her,
putting nickels in the jukebox
to play "Fallen Angel" again and again,
so the music's still going,
somewhere,
later when they find her dead.

Night after night,
I walk through the icy streets
of Cambridge, my home town,
the city I was born in. The neon
sign at the Holiday Inn is always
half-lit. In the bars, people
smoke cigarettes as if their lives
were a Fifties movie, and cancer
and coronaries couldn't afflict them.
Lucky for me
this town shows so many old movies.
I keep busy, work all day,
eat grains and vegetables, feed my cats,
swipe a sponge across the counters—
then, the entertainment. I know
there's something out there shady enough
to keep keeping me distracted.

LISTENING TO BASEBALL IN THE CAR

This morning I argued with a friend
about angels. I didn't believe
in his belief in them—I can't
believe they're not a metaphor.
Our argument, affectionate,
lacking in animus, went nowhere.
We promised to talk again soon.
Now, when I'm driving away
from Boston and the Red Sox
are losing, I hear the announcer
say, "No angels in the sky today"—
baseball-ese for *a cloudless afternoon*,
no shadows to help a man
who waits in the outfield
staring into the August sun.
Although I know the announcer's
not a rabbi or sage (no,
he's a sort of sage, disconsolate
philosopher of batting slumps
and injuries), still I scan
the pale blue sky through my
polarized windshield, fervently
hopeful for my fading team
and I feel something a little
foolish, a prayerful throbbing
in my throat and remember
being told years ago that men
are only little lower than
the angels. Floating ahead of me

at the Vermont border, I see
a few wispy horsemane clouds
which I quietly pray will drift
down to Fenway Park where
a demonic opponent has just
slammed another Red Sox pitch,
and the center fielder—call him Jim—
runs back, back, back,
looking heavenward,
and is shielded and doesn't lose
the white ball in the glare.

TO RTSL, 1985

"I'm drained," the last words, I think, you said
to me, four months before your death, the after-reading
crowd at Harvard lingering for a little piece of you.
Is peace to a heroic sufferer possible in the afterlife
promised by yesterday's priest at the latest funeral?
As the congregation rose, responded, and collapsed,
a crazy redhead derelict poked at my neck
with a leathery Book of Common Prayer. I deserved
it, so I didn't turn around to hiss or beg him off—
I didn't love the deceased and shuddered in failed
grief at the homily's stuffy heavenbound platitudes.

In my pew, Jewish mourners snuffled, rebuffed again
at the restricted Gates of Heaven—no everlasting
Paradise for us. Or fear of Hell. You said you wanted
words meat-hooked from the living steer. You'd miss
them in that sermon but sing a fervent Amazing Grace.
Cal, the students come, no less callow or careerist now;
their dented sensibilities might have offended
or amused you no less than Attila's or your son's
babysitter's views. Had you lived beyond that Yellow
Cab ride, you'd be nearly seventy, more frizzled,
your generation's humble chivalrous relentless pride.

from Nightfire (1978)

BASEBALL

The game of baseball is not a metaphor
and I know it's not really life.
The chalky green diamond, the lovely
dusty brown lanes I see from airplanes
multiplying around the cities
are only neat playing fields.
Their structure is not the frame
of history carved out of forest,
that is not what I see on my ascent.

And down in the stadium,
the veteran catcher guiding the young
pitcher through the innings, the line
of concentration between them,
that delicate filament is not
like the way you are helping me,
only it reminds me when I strain
for analogies, the way a rookie strains
for perfection, and the veteran,
in his wisdom, seems to promise it,
it glows from his upheld glove,

and the man in front of me
in the grandstand, drinking banana
daiquiris from a thermos,
continuing through a whole dinner
to the aromatic cigar even as our team
is shut out, nearly hitless, he is
not like the farmer that Auden speaks of

in Breughel's Icarus,
or the four inevitable woman-hating
drunkards, yelling, hugging
each other and moving up and down
continually for more beer

and the young wife trying to understand
what a full count could be
to please her husband happy in
his old dreams, or the little boy
in the Yankees cap already nodding
off to sleep against his father,
program and popcorn memories
sliding into the future,
and the old woman from Lincoln, Maine,
screaming at the Yankee slugger
with wounded knees to break his leg

this is not a microcosm,
not even a slice of life

and the terrible slumps,
when the greatest hitter mysteriously
goes hitless for weeks, or
the pitcher's stuff is all junk
who threw like a magician all last month,
or the days when our guys look
like Sennett cops, slipping, bumping
each other, then suddenly, the play
that wasn't humanly possible, the Kid

we know isn't ready for the big leagues,
leaps into the air to catch a ball
that should have gone downtown
and coming off the field is hugged
and bottom-slapped by the sudden
sorcerers, the winning team

the question of what makes a man
slump when his form, his eye,
his power aren't to blame, this isn't
like the bad luck that hounds us,
and his frustration in the games
not like our deep rage
for disappointing ourselves

the ballpark is an artifact,
manicured, safe, "scene in an Easter egg,"
and the order of the ball game,
the firm structure with the mystery
of accidents always contained,
not the wild field we wander in,
where I'm trying to recite the rules,
to repeat the statistics of the game,
and the wind keeps carrying my words away